A Tour of Italian Gardens

A Tour of Italian Gardens

JUDITH CHATFIELD

Photographs by
LIBERTO PERUGI

Ward Lock Limited • London

First published in Great Britain in 1988 by
Ward Lock Limited, 8 Clifford Street, London
W1X 1RB, an Egmont Company.

British Library Cataloguing in Publication Data

Chatfield, Judith
  A tour of Italian gardens.
  1. Italy. Gardens to 1960
  I. Title
  712'.6'0945

ISBN 0-7063-6709-X

Designed by Emsworth Studios, New York
Maps by Lundquist Design
Set in type by David E. Seham Associates Inc.
Printed and bound in Japan

Front jacket: *Boboli Garden, Florence*
Back jacket: *Villa Pisani, Stra*
Frontispiece: *Villa Gamberaia, Settignano*

Contents

Preface

This book is intended as an introduction to the classical Italian garden. It is a selective tour, highlighting some of the more important landscape designs that remain in the Italian style. Most of the gardens included are state or city owned and open to the public on a regular basis. For others it is advisable to write the owners and request a visit. Many of the gardens in Tuscany can be visited during the spring and early summer with the Agritourist organization based in Florence. When they have appeared to be regular, I have noted opening days, although Italian schedules are always subject to change.

Several of the gardens have historic importance but do not merit a visit from the casual admirer of Italian gardens because only the "bare bones" or site of the garden survive: Colorno and Venaria Reale are in this category. Attempts are being made to restore the structures of Palazzo Doria and Villa Regina; if they are carried out with time and care, in the future they will be of great interest. At the present their condition is deplorable, yet I included these villas of Genoa and Turin because it is important to show regional gardens in areas formerly rich in major sixteenth- and eighteenth-century gardens, as proven by the old prints and descriptions. I have worked from firsthand observation and from photographs and prints which record the transformations and, alas, deterioration over the years. Gardens photographed at the turn of the century such as Villa d'Este at Tivoli and the Vatican Gardens have been improved with time and more attentive care. Georgina Masson's classic book written in the late 1950s included photographs of gardens then beautifully maintained that have been subsequently neglected. Villa Crivelli at Inverigo has been totally untended and is now in the care of a nearly blind caretaker who unlocks the gate oblivious to the smashed windows and weeds. Masson's description of the secret garden at Villa Rizzardi conjures up a paradise; however, in the two years since the count died, the garden lacks a head gardener, the fountains no longer play, and the beds are not replanted.

Many gardens have in part undergone transformations, so they are not strictly in the Italian style, for example, Marlia, Torrigiani, and Mansi near Lucca, for which projects in classical Italian style exist at variance with their English parklike appearance today. Others in the Veneto and Lombardy border on French taste due to the strong eighteenth-century French influence in these regions. Yet it must be remembered that French gardens derive ultimately from Italian models, the difference lying in the French emphasis on the horizontal as opposed to a vertical perspective axis.

Charles VIII returned from his Neapolitan campaign in 1495 full of enthusiasm for Italian gardens. This was reinforced by the export of Italian gardeners to the courts of the two Florentine-born Medici queens of France, Marie and Catherine. The new imported elements were easily adapted to suit the flat character of the French landscape.

Gardens are extremely fragile works of art, subject to freaks of weather, man's indifference to his ancestors' creations, and finally vandalism. To maintain them today is a costly and time-consuming endeavor. I pay tribute to those owners who do so. As works of art, gardens are rarely studied. Fortunately they are sometimes listed on the rolls of the Belli Arte and hence protected from radical transformation. (How many gardens Italy lost irretrievably to the nineteenth-century craze for English landscape gardens!) Regrettably, public apathy and bureaucracy allow many gardens to deteriorate dangerously. It is to be hoped that there will be a renewed interest in this art form within Italy, and that eventually the Italian government will provide incentives to assist owners of historic gardens to continue this splendid tradition.

J. C.

Introduction

Imperial Roman Gardens

Pleasure gardens first appeared in Italy late in the second century B.C. Hellenistic trading settlements along the Italian coast imported Greek artists, and their work strongly influenced the Roman arts.

Our knowledge of Greek gardens is sketchy, at best based on descriptions by Aristotle and Theophrastus, with hints from relief carvings and vase paintings. We know that the Greeks planted sacred groves to their gods, and Greek scholars had an affinity for gardens; Plato's Academy had a colonnaded *palaestra* with shady walks to combine philosophical discussions with exercise. (The Renaissance took note of this.) The first botanical garden existed by the third century B.C. Alexander the Great's campaigns stimulated an interest in foreign plants and gardens, especially in the Persian "paradise" gardens—half devoted to pleasure and half to the hunt. For the most part, private gardens were utilitarian, restricted to vegetables and herbs. Flowers were reserved for religious rites.

The Romans have left us more tangible traces of their gardens at Tivoli, Pompeii, Herculaneum, Piazza Armerina in Sicily, as well as the Villa of Faustinius on the Tyrrhenian coast. Garden descriptions by the two Plinys, Varro, and Cicero are also of great value.

Pompeiian gardens made the most of a limited enclosed space that insured privacy. These houses usually had an atrium or courtyard for the public at the entrance. This led by a corridor into a private central courtyard called a peristyle, usually bordered with columns, often with a small fishpond or fountain in the center, in which case it was called a *viridarium.* This was on an axis with the living room, which, if space permitted, opened beyond onto the *xystus,* or flower garden. The *xystus* was bordered by box hedges, planted with flowers, ivy, and topiary, and often had a mosaic-decorated fountain niche with a loggia at the far end, or a small stepped fountain cascade. It was not uncommon for the loggia to have an illusionistic wall painting which extended the space with an imaginary landscape. Many of these mural paintings have been discovered in excavations, providing rich information about Roman garden tastes.

Within the villa, rooms were frescoed with architectural landscape scenes of elaborate homes with roof gardens, or were painted to resemble gardens with bird-filled trees, fences, and fountains. Augustus Caesar's wife, Livia, had a subterranean room at Porta Prima, which was a cool, windowless retreat; the enclosing walls were adorned with painted paired pines, oaks, and spruces, interspersed with fruit trees, poppies, periwinkles, irises, and roses behind a balustrade. Birds abounded in the branches.

The ancient Romans loved plant material for its ornamental possibilities. Linked with their deep feeling for the countryside, this affection encouraged the extensive creation of gardens before the fifth-century invasion by the Vandals. The Romans aimed for an orderly garden built on a symmetrical axis with interpenetration of house and garden. The closely linked inner courtyard gardens and living rooms, which then led through a loggia into the *xystus*, would strongly influence the gardens of the Renaissance. There was also an appreciation of the juxtaposition of formal, contained garden and the untamed, surrounding countryside.

Varro's *De re rustica* describes his country home at Cassino, detailing the streams and paths. The *villa rustica* was a working farmhouse as opposed to the *villa urbana* (a house built outside of a city, or in the country as a pleasure house).

Another famed Roman garden lover, Lucullus, had a lavish garden at Cape Miseno near Baiae, another over what are now the Spanish Steps in Rome, and a third at Tusculum, for which he imported fruit trees from Asia Minor. Like Pliny, he had houses for different seasons. When Pompey protested that his house at Tusculum was not suitable for year-round living, Lucullus replied, "What, then, do you think I have not as much sense as the cranes and the storks, who change their habitations with the seasons?" (Varro, *De re rustica*).

In the first century A.D., Pliny the Younger, nephew of the great naturalist, described his various properties in letters to his friends. His *villa urbana* at Laurentum, a winter residence on the seacoast, sixteen miles outside of Rome, is the most appealing. Here the villa and its gardens were sited to enjoy the sea breezes and the views. Covered pathways shielded against blazing sun or strong winds. There were two dining rooms with shades to pull according to weather conditions; one overlooked the sea, the other a sheltered *xystus*. His private apartments were located at the end of the long terrace with a solarium for privacy and quiet when the rest of the household was celebrating Saturnalia. The flower garden was bordered with box hedges, rosemary, and plants pleasant to walk upon in bare feet. Figs, mulberries, and grape vines grew on the property. A grander summer property at Tusculum had a hippodrome in front of the villa for running or exercising horses, surrounded by double rows of plane trees. Alongside was a *gestatio* (or broad pathway) decorated with topiary spelling out Pliny's name, for promenades in litters carried by slaves. The adjacent flower gardens harbored a large dining portico. Another dining area was located along an acanthus and topiary walk. Here the dining table was a fountain with floating dishes. Opposite, a marble pavilion with couch and windows provided respite for cool naps in a "very agreeable gloominess" (Pliny the Younger, *Letter to Apollinaris*). Another portion had a labyrinth. In addition he had a *lucus*, or sacred grove, with temples dedicated to the pagan deities. Beyond were views of the untouched countryside. This was typical of the large country estates, which often had over one thousand acres. Fruits and flowers were raised in hothouses. Fruit trees were often planted in a *quincunx* pattern of alternating rows so that they appear to be planted in five directions. Generally there was a large peristyle entrance court.

Pliny had two additional villas on Lake Como named "Comoedia" and "Tragoedia." These were probably on the sites of Villa Pliniana near Lario,

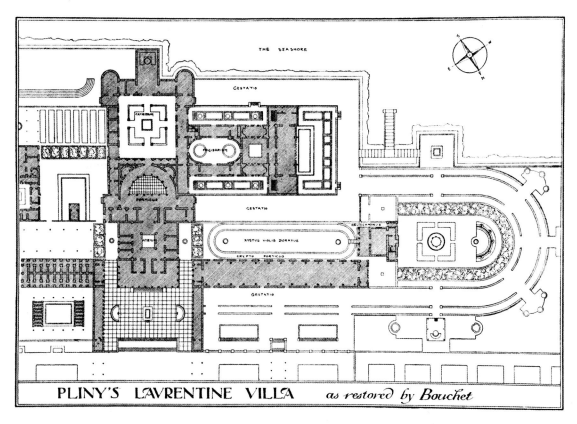

Pliny's Laurentine Villa, from Triggs, *Art of Garden Design . . .* (1906).

which is described by Pliny as set on the water's edge with a spring that surged at regular intervals, and Villa Serbelloni, above Bellagio on the promontory overlooking both branches of Lake Como.

If Pliny's descriptions give us a good idea of patrician gardens, the excavations of Hadrian's villa at Tivoli open our eyes to what Nero's Golden House and Tiberius's gardens on Capri must have been like. The scale is overpowering, expressing the might of the Roman empire. Its aim was to impress and to house a multitude of courtiers, slaves, and large lavish entertainments. Hadrian's villa is a hodgepodge assortment of buildings inspired by the the emperor's travels, and sited to get views and maximum benefit of the sun, without relating one structure to the next. Hadrian was a compulsive collector, favoring Greek art above all others. The buildings here were planned to house his enormous collections. The remains of an immense painted portico, the Pecile, stand alone. Excavations have revealed a large garden, the so-called Stadium, which had many fountains, including a huge one that cascaded down a semicircular series of steps. His fascination with water in the many pools, baths, and fountains without a doubt influenced the planning of the nearby sixteenth-century Villa d'Este's famed fountains. In a small valley is Hadrian's imitation of the Canopus, a temple to the god Serapis, which stood by the Nile at the head of the canal. Here the canal is 390 feet long and surrounded by a graceful arcade on three sides; at the end is a marble *nymphaeum*. In the midst of all this grandeur, Hadrian had a private retreat on an intimate scale consisting of a walled, round pool. Within the pool was a small island measuring about eighty-two feet in diameter, which was reached by two retractable drawbridges. On this island were several small irregularly shaped rooms for study or rest, insuring total privacy.

In his *Natural History* the elder Pliny extols the beauty of the umbrella pine, and informs us that cypress, laurel, myrtle, and plane trees were commonly used in gardens, the cypress often shaped. We learn that box, ivy, ferns, and acanthus provided a foil to the blooms of rockets, lilies, narcissus, violets, verbena, anemones, poppies, hyacinths, oleanders, crocuses, and twelve kinds of roses.

As summers were typically blistering, Roman gardens featured primarily spring flowers. Because of this, importance was placed on evergreens, statuary, fountains, and fishponds. The highest-ranking garden slave was the *topiarius,* who clipped the evergreens in elaborate forms; at times he was permitted to sign his name in boxwork alongside that of the owner's. The *aquarius* was the slave in charge of the fountains and the waterworks. To escape the heat, subterranean rooms were built, such as that of the empress Livia. Within the gardens the artificial grotto appeared, excavated against a hillside or built into a wall, its surface covered with moss, shells, and fake stalactite called *spugne,* usually in rough pumice or tufa. Often a small fountain trickled, heightening the sensation of a cool, refreshing retreat. Sometimes natural grottoes were adapted. The most elaborate natural grotto to come down to us is the cave of Tiberius at Terracina on the Tyrrhenian Sea. A large cavern with smaller adjoining chambers, it was once decorated in glass mosaic, stucco-relief, and statuary. The main grotto contains a spring-fed pool, about seventy-five feet in diameter. Beyond the grotto entrance is a group of smaller rectangular pools, fed with fresh water from the large pool. These were probably for fish that were caught, prepared, and served within the grotto. Tacitus relates how rocks fell upon the diners while Tiberius was there, and his close advisor Sejanus shielded the emperor with his body. Tiberius, undaunted, constructed other grotto chambers for his Capri villas. Found only in 1957, the grotto at Terracina contains shattered fragments of large statuary groups by Hellenistic sculptors from Rhodes. It is thought that the groups depicted Odysseus, Ganymede, possibly a Laocoön, and the Argos—the ship of Jason and the Argonauts in search of the Golden Fleece.

In Rome itself, the zone of the Pincian Hill had the greatest concentration of important gardens and was known as the *collis horticulorum.* The elaborate terminal fountains of the aqueducts became prototypes for Baroque fountains. In the city, potted plants adorned balconies, courtyards, and flat rooftops; trellises appeared on the roof terraces, and small pools and fountains decorated courtyards, just as they do today.

Medieval Gardens

It is only thanks to the monastic orders that the horticultural knowledge amassed by the ancient Romans was preserved. After the destruction of Rome in the fifth century, people barricaded themselves within fortified castles and hill towns; space became too limited for pleasure gardens; at most a small area would be set off for herbs and vegetables. The foundation of monastic rule began at Monte Cassino under San Benedetto in the sixth century. The monastery was conceived of as an independent entity, totally self-sufficient, providing for all the needs of its community. A detailed plan of the large monastery of Saint Gall in Switzerland, dating from the beginning of the tenth century, shows a mix of flowers and herbs in the physic garden. Rue, rosemary, sage, roses, lilies, and gladioli were grown. Herbs were cultivated for medicinal purposes, flowers for ornamenting the altar. Some of the cloisters had fishponds to supply the table for Lenten and fast days. The arcaded cloister was a direct outgrowth of the Roman peristyle courtyard. Occasionally these cloister gardens had an extension of the arcade built as a loggia with seats into the courtyard, such as appears at Monreale in Sicily. The cloister was usually divided into four beds with paths around a central well or fountain; herbs and a few flowers, notably roses and lilies, were grown here. Church cloisters were places for contemplation and peace, and not intended to be utilitarian. A monastery had other areas outside its walls for vegetable plots, flower and herb beds, orchards, and a cemetery.

Some cloisters attached to churches within Rome have been preserved in their original state. The thirteenth-century cloister of the Santi Quattro Coronati has a true garden with roses, camellias, and date palms in the corners. The only ornamentation is the geometric pattern on the vaults of the connecting arches between the plain small sets of columns. In the center is a twelfth-century fountain, unique in Rome. Geraniums, a modern touch, are in pots on the second story. Two large cloisters of the early thirteenth century are found within the basilicas of San Giovanni Laterano and San Paolo fuori le Mura. They both have pairs of twisted, ornamented columns in varying styles, with colored mosaic and marble. Their gardens are planted with box hedges and flowers. Today the church cloister in the midst of a turbulent city comes as a blessed relief from the noise and heat, a place that is inviting to linger and meditate in.

Castles had a small area set aside for the women to grow their herbs for medicinal, dye, and spice purposes. As chivalry developed, the garden enclosure became a focus for discussions of courtly love, and for games such as chess, played standing up around a table. In some of these medieval pleasure gardens, a *piscina* appears for bathing. Simple turf-covered, raised benches were provided to sit or lean back upon. Our knowledge of these gardens is based on miniatures and on frescoes such as Orcagna's *Dance of Death* at Pisa. The interior of a castle was dark, cold, and odiferous; how welcome a sunny patch of garden filled with sweet smelling flowers and herbs must have been to the men and women of the Middle Ages!

During this period, a comprehensive symbolism was developed by the church regarding flowers. The Madonna lily denoted purity; the iris was a symbol of the Queen of Heaven; there was also the red rose of martyrdom, the white rose of purity, the cyclamen of the bleeding sorrow in Mary's heart, the carnation of pure love, the violets of humility, and so forth.

A popular theme in painting was the Madonna of Humility, in which the Virgin is seated on a cushion upon a carpet of flowers within an enclosed garden, the *hortus conclusus*. The concept of the *hortus conclusus* goes back to the Song of Solomon: "A garden enclosed is my sister, my spouse." Stefano da Verona's *Madonna of the Rose Garden* in the Civico Museo d'Arte in Verona shows a typical Madonna of this type. She is seated amid clover (symbol of the Trinity) and red roses; the garden is bordered on three sides by an arched arbor, covered with red and white roses. A small wattle fence is at the bottom; in the upper right-hand corner is a four-lobed pedestal fountain representing the Fountain of Life. A multitude of angels and birds hovers around the Virgin and Child. Later medieval gardens, such as the Visconti's at Pavia, have aviaries to contain rare birds such as those depicted here. The Saracen Emirs, who occupied Sicily from the ninth through the eleventh centuries, continued the tradition of the pleasure parks there. None survive, but the Norman conquerors maintained the concept to a degree, including the custom of setting aside areas for fragrant groves of lemons and oranges, which would become prevalent elsewhere during the Renaissance. The Saracen-Norman gardens had a preserve for wild animals and birds and made much use of water in reflecting ponds, fountains, and channels for irrigation. Emperor Frederick II in Southern Italy had a number of gardens; however, his model was not the Islamic style, which pervaded Sicily, but that of the ancient Romans. He aspired to revive the Roman Empire and emulated Roman taste, placing antique statuary in his gardens. Aside from its use in the gardens of the ruler of Naples as recounted by Boccaccio, antique statuary was not used in gardens. It was apt to be destroyed to make lime with the excuse of its improper pagan content, although a sculpted piece occasionally found its way into a medieval garden atop a fountain shaft.

The fullest descriptions of medieval gardens are found in Pietro de' Crescenzi's eighth book of the *Opus ruralium commodorum: Libro dell'agricoltura* first issued in Latin in 1305, successively published in Italian, German, and French; and illustrated in the fifteenth century. This is the only agricultural treatise that has come down to us from this period. (There were herbals perpetuated by the monasteries and also compiled by lay persons.) Pietro de' Crescenzi carefully read Roman garden authorities, such as Varro, Palladius, and Cato, before setting down instructions for designing gardens for three classes: the "people of moderate means and according to their social position," for the nobles, and for the king.

For the common people he prescribed a garden of two to four acres. All gardens, he stated, should be planted on flat ground with square beds for flowers and herbs. A moat should surround the garden, or it should be bordered with high walls, or hedged with roses or fruit trees. Each garden should have a fountain in the center, turf seats, and a vine pergola for shade. The plants included were mint, rue, marjoram, sage, basil, roses, gladioli, lilies, violets, corn lilies, as well as cypresses, pomegranates, bays, apples, and pears. The elaborated garden had briar hedges, a large orchard, an arched trellis, and an outer hedge of pomegranates for hot climates, hazel or quince for cooler zones.

The princely garden was strongly based on the Sicilian gardens, parklike in its dimensions of at least twenty square acres. A complex network of a central fountain with water channels irrigating all areas of the garden was suggested. Equally spaced rows of orange and lemon trees took their place with pines, cypresses, and palms. All details were to be on a larger scale than the lesser categories of gardens—grander hedges, pergolas, and pavilions. Wildlife was to graze in view of the villa, and copper-netted trees would confine birds. A fine lawn was to be centered with a pillared fountain; other fountains were to be found in pergolas or pillared pavilions.

He gave instructions for interlacing tree branches and bushes to create shelters and rustic seats.

The emphasis is on pleasure and an appeal to the senses—the songs of birds, the trickling of water, the perfume of the citrus and the roses, the vision of beauty in nature. Such a garden is the Palazzo Rufolo at Ravello, which retains its medieval character. Its open double loggia was used for entertaining and looks over a small garden on the edge of a cliff with a view of the Amalfi coast. This is a rare medieval private garden dating from the thirteenth century. Its encrusted polychrome loggia is of Arab-Sicilian style.

The early humanists of the fourteenth century mention personal pleasure gardens. Dante's family had a small garden at their house at Camerata. Boccaccio in his preface to the "Third Day" of the *Decameron* describes in detail a villa garden above Florence with its fountain, flowering field, and dining loggia. Petrarch, the first medieval man known to climb a mountain in order to enjoy the view, had a small garden at his last house at Arqua. The house still stands: an outer staircase rises from the small front garden of clipped box hedges. The rear has fruit trees and shady paths. Petrarch died here in 1374 sitting at his desk by a window overlooking the valley and the Euganean hills. He described in more detail another garden he created in Parma in 1348 with a lawn, and an orchard with pears, plums, and apples, together with rosemary and hyssop. Here he successfully grafted foreign vines.

Early Renaissance Gardens

De re aedifactoria, written around 1450 by Leon Battista Alberti, had a great influence on fifteenth-century Florentine garden design. Alberti borrowed heavily from the precepts of Vitruvius and the letters of Pliny regarding the siting of the villa on a hillside for the advantages of healthy air, sunshine, and views. The site should, he wrote, encompass a view of "... the town, the country, the sea, or a wide expanse and the familiar tops of the hills and mountains." The loggia, he advised, should be placed to catch the sun in winter and the shade in scorching summer. It was also to provide access to the garden, and hence the revival of the concept of inter-linking house and garden which becomes paramount in gardens of the Renaissance villas. Like Pliny, he urges the use of topiary and paths planted with regular rows of cherry trees or pomegranates garlanded with roses, and cypresses wound with ivy. He fully describes how grottoes should be constructed of a spongy stone (pumice or travertine), green wax, and shellwork. Statuary, he warns, may be humorous, but must be decorous. He neglects to mention large-scale architectural garden structures, nor is there any reference to the use of an axial plan.

Alberti designed the trend-setting Palazzo Rucellai in Florence in 1446. It is very likely that his garden theories were considered for another Rucellai property built about thirteen years later on the outskirts of Florence at Quaracchi. Bernardo Rucellai left detailed accounts of this garden, which was built on a gentle rise with a view from the loggia of a tree-bordered avenue stretching to the Arno on a central axis. The house was moated with fishponds for decoration (not defense by this date). An arbor extended from the house, flanked by straight box-hedged paths and orchards to an enclosed garden, a *giardino segreto,* where the family could retreat in privacy out of view of the passersby. Herbs, flowers, and topiary works grew around a lawn in the garden. Beyond this the allée commenced, continuing to the banks of the river. By 1480 the local people felt so strongly about the importance of this garden that they were deeded it and promised to preserve it at their own expense. (No trace remains today.)

The introduction of axial plans, albeit to a partial degree at this time, reflects the fascination of the fifteenth-century Renaissance artists with discoveries in portraying perspective. The eye was to be led gradually from the foreground of the garden to the far distance.

Alberti was not concerned with an overall coherent garden plan. Only in the writings of the architect-sculptor Francesco di Giorgio (from about 1482) is the imposition of a complete geometric garden design insisted upon, "to make the garden into some perfect figure, as circular, square or three cornered, next to these come the pentagon, hexagonal, octagonal. . . ." *(Trattato di architettura civile e militare).*

The great fantasy garden of the fifteenth century is described in the *Hypnerotomachia Poliphili* by Francesco Colonna, a Dominican monk, written around 1467 and printed with woodcut illustrations in 1499 by the

Scene from F. Colonna, *Hypnerotomachia Poliphili* (15th century).

Aldine Press in Venice. It describes the dream of Poliphilus who wanders with his loved one through a landscape consisting of concentric circles, the segments of which are portions of the garden on the island of Cytherea. At the center is the Fountain of Venus surrounded by red marble screens held together with white marble pillars. Each area is treated in an original manner, with orchards, and woods of different trees, vegetable gardens, meadows, and formal gardens. It is unusual as it identifies in surprising detail for its time, the abundant variety of flowers. Contemporary accounts are generally vague in listing the precise flowers grown in gardens. An exception is Botticelli's *Primavera,* in which the painter lovingly portrays forty different identifiable flowers growing around Florence in the spring. The *Hypnerotomachia* is a compendium of garden structures, fountain designs, pergolas, and peristyles, with complex designs of knotted flower beds. An amphitheater becomes a tiered flower garden, inspired no doubt by the tomb of Augustus in Rome. The entire garden is on a flat plain, surrounded by a river and a clipped hedge of myrtle and cypresses. Possibly for the first time, plants were utilized as architectural building material. Ahead of his time, Colonna thoroughly sprinkles his gardens with antique ruins, altars, and statuary. The interest in Roman visual arts trailed behind that of its literature and sciences. In the fifteenth century statuary is gradually incorporated into gardens independently of architectural construction. Lorenzo il Magnifico had a sculpture garden near San Marco in Florence where artists, including the young Michelangelo, were encouraged to study antique models.

Superb sculptors including Donatello, Bernardo Rossellino, and Andrea del Verrocchio were commissioned to produce pieces for Florentine gardens. The charming putto grasping a slippery fish, now in the Palazzo Vecchio, was made for a fountain at Cosimo de' Medici's villa at Careggi. Donatello's *Judith and Holofernes* was part of a fountain for the Palazzo Medici in Via Larga.

The fifteenth-century garden is well represented in paintings of the Annunciation or *sacra conversazione.* Fra Angelico's gardens are neat, with paneled marble walls or simple wooden picket fences, rows of cypresses, and an abundance of terra-cotta potted plants. His lawns are carpeted with flowers. Botticelli and Mantegna invent intricately interlaced bowers framing their Madonnas. Andrea Mantegna, Fra Angelico, and Fra Filippo Lippi all show flat-topped wooden trellises in their gardens and on rooftops.

The Medici prospered first as wool merchants, then as international bankers, to become politically the most powerful family in Florence. The early Medici ruled by well-placed influence, in time supplying popes from their family. Later Medici openly held power and were created grand dukes. Florence flowered under their patronage of arts and letters. The head of the line, Cosimo, Pater Patrie, had the foresight to hire Michelozzo Michelozzi as his architect to create country villas at Careggi and Cafaggiolo, in addition to his city palazzo in Via Larga. Via Larga's garden is now much reduced in size, but a detailed record of it from the fifteenth century survives in which great emphasis was placed on its topiary creations. These depicted "elephants, a wild boar, a ship with sails, a ram, a hare with its ears up, a wolf fleeing from dogs, an antlered deer." Elaborate topiary was more popular in the city gardens than the country villas. Cosimo's remodeled villa at Careggi featured a two-story loggia, which juts out into the garden for dining and admiring the view. Here the famed Platonic Academy met to discuss philosophy. Cosimo died at Careggi in 1464.

The Villa Medici at Fiesole was also built by Michelozzo, for Cosimo's son, Giovanni. Here is an early example of a terraced hillside garden, but one that does not take advantage of the site to create dramatic or coherent linking features; the different levels are accessible by indirect paths, or through the basement doors of the villa. (Scenographic linking of hillside levels must wait for the sixteenth- and seventeenth-century developments in Rome.) However, Michelozzo has paid attention to Alberti, siting the villa on a hillside with sweeping views of the city set in the river valley below. Also here, more so than at Careggi, he has achieved a happy inter-blending of house and garden, again using a loggia. Here it is open, on an axis with the top terrace garden.

A city garden built on courtyard terraces was naturally restricted in area, but was occasionally planned to encompass views beyond its balustrades. That of the Palazzo Piccolomini in Pienza has retained its fifteenth-century appearance with a triple-tiered loggia overlooking a small box parterre with simple central fountain and a view of the hills of Tuscany beyond. The Montefeltros at Urbino had a terrace garden with marble seats set against the walls. Loggias such as that of Palazzo Strozzi in Florence were sometimes transformed into roof gardens with potted plants and perhaps a fountain.

Gardens in Tuscany—with the exception of the sixteenth-century Pratolino and Boboli—remained reticent in character well into subsequent centuries. The scale of the surrounding hillsides is more to the measure of man; the temperament of the Tuscans, so attuned to their landscape, is less rhetorical than that of the Romans, more privately oriented. As a rule, one does not find the theatricality of site, use of water, or vastness of the Roman gardens in Tuscany. Gardens in Tuscany are more intimate, more akin to the medieval garden, often consisting merely of the *giardino segreto* surrounded by orchards and meadows.

Later Italian Gardens

By the sixteenth century, nothing was left to chance, unplanned, or temporary in garden design. All was firmly connected and balanced. The Tuscan gardens of Castello, Celsa, and Vicobello were created in the first half of the sixteenth century. Celsa and Vicobello are small private gardens near Siena; Castello is a Medici villa on the outskirts of Florence. All three follow basic principles of Italian garden design, which persisted through the centuries. Renaissance symmetry, based on opposing solid forms separated by open spaces, dictates that in the immediate vicinity of the villa there should be a cleared area, or open terrace, setting apart a flower parterre from the villa. In the distance, higher hedges or trees mark off the parterre zone and act as a foil to the villa. By placing the parterre in proximity to the villa, its pattern could be enjoyed from the upper windows. Often, as at Celsa, a *barco*, or woods for hunting, was situated apart from the villa; eventually the garden will meld with adjacent woods in the Baroque period.

Castello had an elaborate iconographical program, partially realized, setting forth the beneficial rule of the Medici family over Tuscany. It was ahead of its time. Later gardens such as Bomarzo had a more fanciful imagery, much of its meaning now obscured, but of personal import to the garden's creator. Pratolino in the second half of the sixteenth century had a series of theme grottoes, loosely linked together by the idea of water.

By mid-century the educated public was accustomed to complex allegorical theatrical productions and intricate movable stage sets. Bernardo Buontalenti, the Florentine architect and stage designer, turned his fertile imagination to the ingenious grottoes of Pratolino and Boboli.

As the theater moved into gardens, special amphitheaters were planned for gardens such as Boboli and Villa Madama. A century later, smaller villas such as Gori, Marlia, and Garzoni—all in Tuscany—had their own green theaters for private performances.

During the High Renaissance a demand sprang up for lavish buildings for the princes of the Church, attracting the foremost architects of the day: Giacomo Barozzi da Vignola, Bartolommeo Ammanati, Michelangelo, Pirro Ligorio, the Sangallos, Giorgio Vasari, and Donato Bramante, all of whom concerned themselves with garden designs. Pleasure pavilions surrounded by gardens were built for entertainment purposes rather than for habitation because of the threat of malaria. Villa Madama, the Orti Farnesiani, and later Villa Giulia, the Casino Borghese, Villa Pamphili, and the Farnesina all fit this category.

To a much greater degree than in the early Renaissance, architects were concerned with the conception of villa and garden as a unity. Donato Bramante led the way with the Vatican garden of the Belvedere. His job was to unite the Villa Belvedere with the Vatican Palace. They were separated by a wide incline and slightly askew from each other. The problem was brilliantly resolved with a series of three terraces linked by flights of stairs and ramps rising to a large niche as a perspective focal point. The buildings were joined by storied loggias on either side of the open terraces. Bramante's rising perspective design, with its symmetry and proportions, was the culmination of the Renaissance era and point of departure for future gardens. From this time on, gardens became far more architectural in character.

Tuscan gardens, led by Niccolò Tribolo's example at Boboli, used green hedges as construction material to a greater degree than the Romans did. Since the early sixteenth century the Romans tended towards masonry in their gardens. A natural slope was transformed with terraces and flights of stairs. The gardens were grandiose at the expense of intimacy.

Villa Madama with its vari-shaped garden rooms was strung across a hillside to best incorporate views of Rome below; the villa itself opened out by side loggias and courtyards into the garden. Here the interpenetration of garden and villa was exploited to its fullest. Its plans were imitated for Villa Imperiale at Pesaro and for the Palazzo del Tè at Mantua.

Giacomo Barozzi da Vignola's wonderful designs for water-chains appear at Caprarola and at Villa Lante outside of Rome. However, his use of water was timid compared to what was achieved at Frascati. Frascati had an unlimited source of water, which the cardinals harnessed to dramatize their gardens and sent cascading over elaborate "theaters." Villa d'Este at nearby Tivoli is the epitome of fountain art, utilizing water imaginatively in endless variations.

To the north, the Gonzaga and Este families had sophisticated gardens, mostly vanished today. In Mantua the Palazzo del Tè and the hanging gardens of the Palazzo Ducale are rare survivors. The Este court in Ferrara was host to the major pastoral poets of the day including Torquato and Bernardo Tasso, Julius Caesar Scaliger, and Ludovico Ariosto, who wrote *Orlando Furioso* with its images of a talking myrtle tree and a knight who is transformed by Alcina into a plant. A familiarity with symbolism and ancient myths was taken for granted in the gardens of the literate; nymphs inhabited their grottoes and muses peopled their allées.

Wealthy Venetians established secondary residences on the mainland. Andrea Palladio and his follower Vincenzo Scamozzi designed villas for them on the Veneto that functioned also as farms. In 1615 Scamozzi set forth his ideas on garden design in *L'Idea dell'architettura universale.* In it he advocates squares of lawn in front of the villa, and a long approach allée of elms. He discusses fountains at length and insists on the inclusion of fishponds and lemon groves.

The Venetians had a great natural affinity for landscape and color. Flowering plants were used freely, gathered from all over the world. The generally flat terrain simplified designs architecturally, but the layout usually incorporated a view of the surrounding countryside. Few of these gardens survived the fad for English landscape since they were relatively easy to transform.

The North's proximity to France and Savoy rule meant that inevitably French styles filtered through in the eighteenth century. Of course it must be recalled that thanks to the imported Medici queens and their gardens—Marie's at Luxembourg, and Catherine's at the Tuileries—much that was intrinsically Italian influenced French garden design. Years earlier the courtiers of Charles VIII had returned to France filled with admiration for Neapolitan gardens; furthermore there was an impressive group of Italian artists practicing at Fontainebleau.

Broadly, if we are to differentiate between French and Italian garden taste, it must be noted that French gardens are conceived on the horizontal rather than the vertical. The garden is laid out on flat land, the fountains are low to the ground, and water lies in flat sheets. The French effect depends largely on broad parterre patterns as seen from a terrace or window above. These parterres are often in arabesque *broderie* designs without hedges. Avenues tend to be narrow. *Berceaux* (green arbors), and *bosquets* (groves) with *salles cabinets* (garden rooms defined by tall hedges) are featured. These modes were especially prevalent around Turin and Milan.

The gardens of Caserta near Naples, planted after 1750, are a last gasp of Baroque garden design in Italy. The design is basically French in inspiration; however, the cascade, with its forceful flow of water, is entirely Italian.

The real death knell to Italian garden design was the transformation of existing formal gardens into English landscape gardens in the last century. One could insist that even these gardens have their roots in ancient Roman ones—inspired by the landscape frescoes of Pompeii, in imitating the classical ruins and temples that dotted their meadows and woods, or in the paintings of the Roman *campagna* by Claude Lorrain, so admired by the English landscape architect William Kent. If so, Italian garden design has turned full circle.

I Piedmont Lombardy Veneto

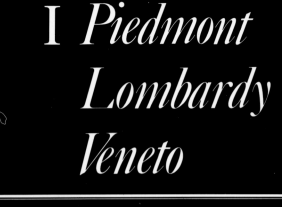

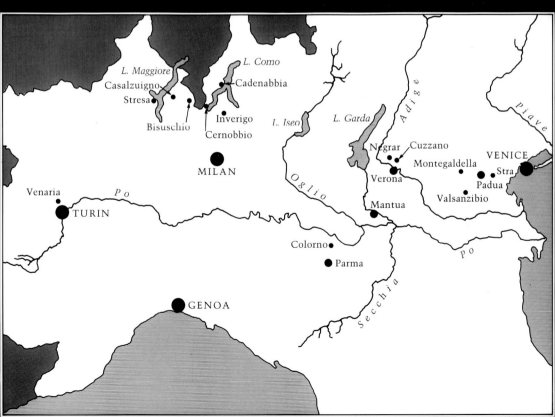

L. Maggiore

L. Como

Casalzuigno
Stresa
Bisuschio
Cernobbio
Inverigo
Cadenabbia

L. Iseo

L. Garda

Adige

Piave

MILAN

Venaria
TURIN

Po

Oglio

Negrar
Cuzzano
Montegaldella
Verona
Valsanzibio
Padua
Stra
VENICE

Mantua

Colorno
Parma

Secchia

Po

GENOA

Villa Regina

Turin
Gardens open upon request:
Assessorato alla piani-
ficazione territoriale e
montagna
Via M. Vittoria, 12
Turin

In 1569 Turin suffered a devastating fire. In the years following, the city was completely replanned on a grid pattern, allowing for a garden for each house. Turin, therefore, is very possibly the first planned "garden city." By the seventeenth century the city was well known for its remarkable Italian-style terraced gardens. Regrettably these are now in pitiful condition. Villa Regina, formerly known as Villa Lodovica or as Villa Vigna di Santa Maria Regina, however, has come down to us in a retrievable condition. Within the city limits, it lies just across the river against the hillside.

Villa Regina was built for Prince Maurizio, son of Carlo Emanuele I. At the age of fourteen Prince Maurizio was made a cardinal but he later renounced his religious orders and married his niece, Lodovica Maria, when she was thirteen, he forty-nine. His villa then became known as Villa Lodovica. It was begun in 1616 following designs for both villa and garden by Ascanio Vittozzi, who had died the previous year. Amadeo di Castella-monte transformed and enlarged the villa later in the same century. The villa hosted many parties, balls, and theatrical presentations, including a musical drama, *La Caccia* by Count Lodovico San Martino d'Agliè in 1620 for Madame Reale, Marie Cristina of France.

Prince Maurizio's real interests were architectural and archaeological. He turned to ancient sources for guidance in his plantings and for the design of the amphitheater. He created the Accademia dei Solinghi, a group of intellectuals that met on the grounds of the villa. After he died of apoplexy in 1657, his wife enlarged and embellished the property with the help of the architect Amadeo di Castellamonte (who had probably also worked for her husband). When she died childless in 1672, the villa passed to King Vittorio Amadeo II, whose wife Anna d'Orléans loved it and placed their coat-of-arms atop the belvedere, renaming it "Villa Vigna di Santa Maria Regina". Filippo Juvarra modernized some of the rooms in 1729.

The villa was inherited by Carlo Emanuele IV, who abdicated in 1796, then by his brother Vittorio Emanuele I upon his return to Italy from Sardinia in 1814. In 1868 the Istituto Nazionale delle Figlie dei Militari received the property from Vittorio Emanuele II. The parterres flanking the villa became playgrounds; today, the young custodian has planted a vegetable garden on the site. No trace remains of the original outlines. A few old school desks and a blackboard remain in the pavilion.

The broad terraces with marble balustrades in front of the villa overlook the city and the Alps beyond. Below is a large round pond with

22 · Piedmont, Lombardy, Veneto

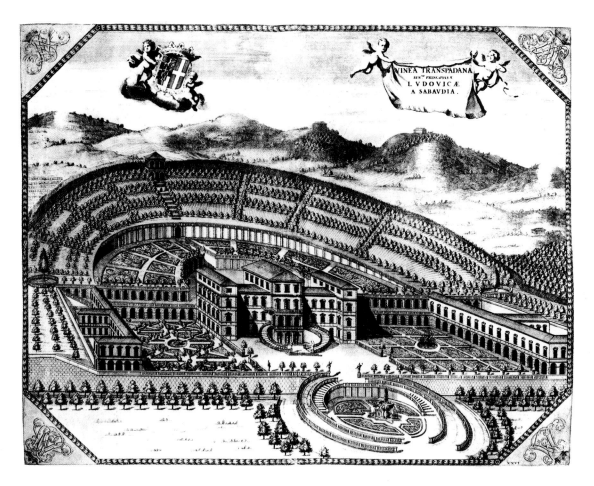

Villa Regina, from *Theatrum Sabaudiae* (1700).

statues of sirens and bearded men sitting along the edges, and a river god in the center. This portion of the garden is set on a lawn with conifers planted in the English style.

In line with the rear facade of the villa are the remains of formal gardens with an amphitheater against the hill. During Prince Maurizio's stay in Rome he visited Villa Aldobrandini and Villa d'Este at Tivoli, which influenced his choice of design. The amphitheater courtyard is semicircular, and rises to a belvedere decorated with niches and a marble balustrade. The niches alternately contain flowerpots and statues of humorous or classical subjects by local sculptors. These apparently replaced antique Roman sculptures that were excavated in the vicinity. In the center of the courtyard is a small, four-lobed basin. The retaining wall of the amphitheater divides at the center into a staircase leading to a grotto set behind a fishpond. This grotto is decorated with mosaics, tufa, and seashells in the shape of angels. A statue of a wild king is flanked by others of youths and matrons in damaged condition. Side stairs lead behind the grotto to a landing marked with obelisks.

A nereid pours water from a vase down twelve center steps. Here is the two-story belvedere facing an oval basin which formerly had statues in

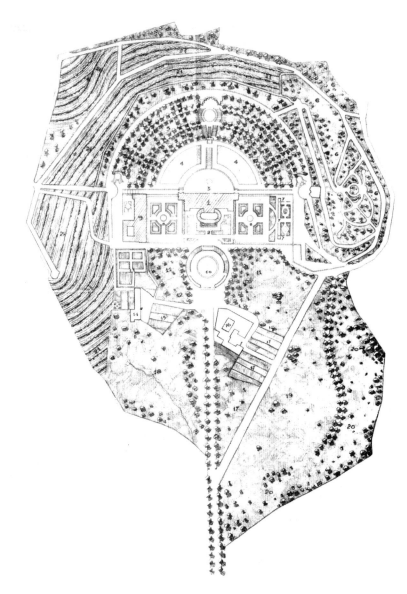

the center. This basin is surrounded by a decorated wall with mask fountains. The stonework of the belvedere and of the lower amphitheater court
has a kinship with Castellamonte's work at Venaria Reale and is in part
attributable to him. One spring on the hilltop provides water for all of the
gardens: underground channels carry the water from the belvedere's fishpond to the nereid's vase, down the water cascades, to finish in the large
pond of the sirens in front of the villa.

The ground floor of the belvedere has niches with three large statues
of mediocre production, and one smaller one—the bust of a woman, probably by Giovanni Battista Bernero. The coroneted Savoy coat-of-arms with
French lilies, which surmounts the belvedere, was added after the depiction
of the belvedere in the *Theatrum Sabaudiae* of 1682, but appears in an

engraving by Baroni di Tavigliano dated 1737. This upper portion with pine trees and balustrade was probably built to the design of Juvarra or Baroni.

The hillside had flower beds and rows of trees. Access roads curved around the amphitheater. Flanking the villa were formal geometric flower beds. A walled passage to the right leads from the villa to the Baroque pavilion, or caffehaus, used by the Accademia dei Solinghi for its meetings. This group attracted the most eminent men in politics, science, letters, and the arts. They read poems and essays here, and strolled along rambling paths under horse chestnuts behind the pavilion. The pavilion itself, which was restored in 1936, is approached by an imposing staircase. The pavilion's facade combines convex and concave surfaces with decorations of tufa, pilasters, balustrades, and a coat-of-arms with the Sabauda cross, and devices of Leon, Castille, and the Bourbon lily.

A complementary structure was projected for the opposite side of the garden. Of this, only a curved base was constructed with a double-ramped staircase against the gentle slope. The base has niches with statues and busts, and is topped by a railing.

The formal portions of the garden were surrounded by woods and vineyards, now all wildly overgrown. One can traipse through the garden pulling aside briars on a narrowly cut path along which strawberries and wildflowers seek the sun. To wander in this garden today is akin to exploring Sleeping Beauty's forest. The basic garden structures are intact, and merit clearing of weeds and destructive ivy. Some restoration work is being done on the villa itself.

Villa Venaria Reale

The most spectacular of Turin's seventeenth-century gardens was that of Villa Venaria Reale, which has all but vanished today. This was built just north of the city around 1600 by Count Amadeo di Castellamonte as a hunting preserve for Duke Carlo Emanuele II. The architect Castellamonte published an imaginary dialogue with Bernini, who was visiting Turin at the time, describing to him in minute detail the villa, its statues, and gardens. This massive villa was in its time one of the most impressive in Piedmont. Engravings from *Theatrum Sabaudiae* show a series of three walled gardens with geometric beds, balustraded retaining walls, an orangerie by Filippo Juvarra, and large architectural arches leading to connecting staircases. Set amid lemon trees in front of the villa was a graceful fountain of Cervio. To the rear of the villa, obelisks mark the gate which faced the elaborate fountain of Hercules riding a dolphin. From a belvedere platform, sweeping horseshoe-shaped stairs ending in small twin towers surmounted a loggia with caryatid figures. The walls of the loggia were decorated by panels encrusted with tufa and rock crystal. Statues adorned the tops of pilasters, and busts were set in niches. Facing the fountain was a long canal terminating in a large balustraded pond with an elaborate wedding-cake construction in the center. Tiers of steps circled the island,

Villa Venaria Reale, from
Theatrum Sabaudiae
(1700).

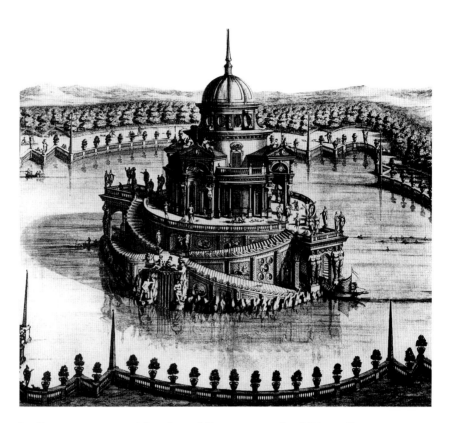

Temple of Diana, Villa
Venaria Reale, from
Theatrum Sabaudiae
(1700).

leading to a terrace with a domed Baroque temple of Diana. Entry was through a portico supported by atlantes of grotesque old men. The pond and canal were spacious enough for navigation. A walled-in hunting park surrounded the villa. Fate was unkind to the Villa Venaria Reale. The French sacked it in 1693. Filippo Juvarra and Benedetto Alfieri restored and enlarged it in 1701 for Carlo Emanuele III, only to have it again damaged by the French five years later. Early in the nineteenth century it was further damaged. Semiderelict, it served as a barracks for the artillery forces of the Italian army. Since 1961 a portion of the building with the entrance clocktowers has been restored. Work continues on the buildings but the garden is completely lost. The restored wing of the palace emphasizes the ruin of the rest. Accompanied by a mangy shepherd dog we climbed the stairs within the castle to view the sites of the former gardens—a rough clearing to the rear, with mountains in the distance, all lush vegetation and forest now where the garden had been. The canal has vanished, as has its lake to the side. The position of the front courtyard fountain has been established, but nothing remains to be seen. The village, however, with its arcaded streets and gatehouse-church lies in charming contrast to the wasted villa and garden.

These two Italian-style gardens of Villa Regina and Villa Venaria Reale are now mere vestiges of their former glory. However, Turin does have two of Italy's purest exercises in French garden design—Palazzo Reale, whose gardens are said to have been planned by Le Nôtre himself; and the gardens of Villa Stupinigi—both accessible to the public.

Isola Bella

Stresa, Lake Maggiore
Gardens open to the public

One of the most extraordinary seventeenth-century Baroque gardens is the famed Isola Bella. Floating like a palatial barge, the island off Stresa on Lake Maggiore is the largest of several owned by the Borromeo family. The garden is an enchanting place, its ten terraces rising like a ship's prow in the reflecting waters. The palace and its adjacent village cover the remaining third of the irregularly shaped island.

Begun in 1632 by Count Carlo Borromeo III, it was originally named Isola Isabella, after his wife; the name has been popularly shortened to Bella, or "beautiful." He leveled the site, working with the architect Angelo Crivelli. The work was continued, and the gardens completed by 1671 under Carlo's sons, Count Vitaliano IV and Gilberto, with the architects Carlo Fontana and Francesco Castelli. Isola Bella was intended as a summer residence. The original project called for a port facing north; this was modified to face northeast next to the retainer's village. The north facade was never completed; in fact, work on portions of the palace continues today. A model of the entire early project is found in a grotto on the ground floor of the palace.

Because of the irregular shape of the island, it was impossible to design the gardens on a straight axis with the palace. Access to the garden is through the tapestry room and into the rounded Courtyard of Diana. At a right angle to the palace, double flights of steps lead up around a niche with Diana's statue, bringing the visitor to the central path of the garden; its position off center to the palace is camouflaged by trees at the top of the courtyard.

Bordering the courtyard to the left is the Theater of Hercules with its large statue set in an oblong garden. And above it is the large parterre originally planted with grass squares, which leads to the water theater rising in five tiers one hundred feet above the level of the lake. This structure conceals a gigantic cistern pumping water for the garden from the lake. The hydraulics for the garden are the work of Mora Torreggia, a Roman. From the balustraded terrace on the top are splendid views of the surrounding garden terraces and the lake. The water theater is decorated with pebble-encrusted pilasters and niches studded with statuary and enormous scallop shells. Potted azaleas line the steps on either side. The whole confection is crowned by a rearing unicorn—family symbol of the Borromeo. Obelisks capped by Prince de Galles plumes dot the upper range of terraces. Statuary in the garden is by Carlo Simonetta and Giuseppe Rusnati.

29 · *Isola Bella*

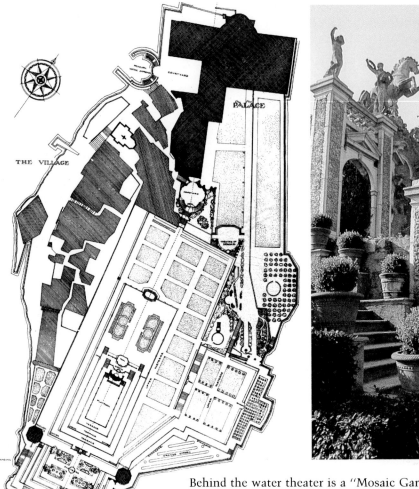

Isola Bella, from Triggs,
Art of Garden Design . . .
(1906).

Behind the water theater is a "Mosaic Garden"—a small formal garden with *broderie* parterres. The pump for the cistern is concealed in one of the two hexagonal marble towers.

Below, to the left of the water theater is a garden of rare flowers and plants with ancient *Laurus camphora*, coffee, tea, bread trees, *Aquilaia saponaria*, orchids, tamarinds, myrtles, *Taxus bacata*, *Strofanto*, rhododendrons, camellias, and cork. Oleanders and azaleas bloom in profusion on the large parterre above. Bordering it are plantations of conifers. Orchids grow in grotto-style greenhouses. The true residents of the garden are a flock of white peacocks, their tails sweeping the paths behind them like bridal veils.

The 1726 print by Marcantonio Dal Re shows the garden quite bare of vegetation. This was in accordance with eighteenth-century taste. In subsequent centuries, the plants have increased and flourished, creating the paradisal hanging gardens that so impressed the French romantics Alfred de Musset and Stendhal.

Visible from the palace windows is the motto in *broderie* planting: "Humilitas"—a blatant contradiction to the lavishness of the island's creation.

In 1685, fourteen years after its completion, Bishop Burnet visited the villa. He calls the Borromean Islands "the loveliest spots of ground in the World, there is nothing in all Italy that can be compared to them, they have the full view of the Lake, and the ground rises so sweetly in them that nothing can be imagined like the Terrasses here" (G. Burnet, *Some Letters*).

In 1739 Charles de Brosses, the French scholar and president of the parliament of Burgundy, described at length the structure of the garden and its fountains, which were not functioning. He concluded that he had never seen such a singular palace so singularly placed; it resembled a fairy tale palace. He spoke of each terrace being covered with oranges, jasmine, or pomegranates.

Napoleon, Josephine, and their entourage of fifty were guests here in August 1797. Banquets, concerts, and dances took place in the garden in their honor.

Isola Bella, from M. A. Dal Re, *Ville di delizia* (1726).

Villa il Bozzolo

Casalzuigno
Gardens open to the public

Villa il Bozzolo is an unusual Lombard example of a measured, stately design using a steep slope and meadows rather than the more characteristic flat gardens of the region. This late seventeenth-century garden is composed of a long approach drive—passing through a gate, across a parterred area, and leading eventually to a series of four stone balustraded terraces. Each terrace terminates in multiple flights of steps framing a large fountain. The view should be seen from this elevated point. Above the fountain is a large, slightly depressed, grassy octagonal clearing, or theater, surrounded by a thick ring of cypresses and woods. A steep path marked by cypresses continues to the summit. The flights here separate in two and are ornamented by statues of putti. The stuccoed villa is placed deliberately to the left, leaving the perspective unbroken. It is linked to the central garden instead by a transverse path, which leads to the terraces as well as to a chapel. A small flower garden is tucked away by the side of the villa for more intimate enjoyment.

The garden is found in the sparsely inhabited Val Cuvia, north of Varese at the small village of Casalzuigno. A large grilled gate with handsome wrought-ironwork frames the perspective from the approach road.

Villa il Bozzolo, from S. Lange, *Ville Italiane; Lombardia* (1984).

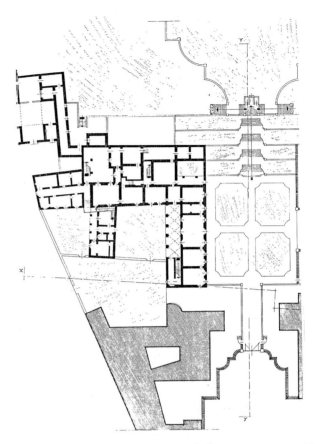

The villa with its vast park was intended as a summer residence. Giroldino della Porta built it in the first half of the sixteenth century; a small garden next to the villa was laid out at that time. His grandson, Gian Angelo II toured the chateaux of France and nearer home studied Isola Bella's design. Later when he brought his bride, Contessa Isabella Giulini to the villa, he redesigned the park, shifting the central axis of the garden at a right angle to the house, to run up against the hillside. The house is hidden from the long axis view. Bensperando II, who inherited the villa around 1670, added to the family wealth, enabling his oldest son Carlo Girolamo, in turn, to add a north wing to the villa before he died in 1704. The villa as it is seen today dates from his time. Carlo Girolamo was one of four brothers who shared it. Together they completed their father's work on the property, adding a church. In 1761 the estate passed to Giuseppe, son of Carlo Girolamo and last of the della Porta line, and hence through his wife's family, the Ferraris. Ultimately it belonged to Professor Camillo Bozzolo, who died in 1920. Professor Bozzolo donated it to the Comune of Casalzuigno.

The sixteenth-century English traveler Thomas Coryat declared Il Bozzolo to be a "passing delectable place of solace." Pink roses, geraniums in pots, and stone putti on the walls soften the architecture of the garden. It is neatly kept with pebble-patterned paths. A grassy field sets off the cypresses, which regrettably are diseased.

Villa Cicogna

Bisuschio
Gardens open to the public
from mid-April to early
November

Little-known towns in Italy often harbor minor treasures. The Lombard Villa Cicogna with its lovely garden is one of these. Located on a steep hillside in the village of Bisuschio, five miles north of Varese, the garden has many sweeping views of the Brevio valley below and Lake Lugano to the northeast.

The villa itself was originally built by the scholar and poet Ascanio Mozzoni as a hunting lodge with a preserve rich in deer and bears. In the main salon there is a life-size terra-cotta statue of a hunting dog who threw himself at a bear that was on the verge of attacking Galeazzo Maria Sforza, the duke of Milan. The event took place here soon after 1450. The dog was killed, but there is a tomb in his memory in the park of the property. Galeazzo Maria continued to visit the brothers Agostino and Antonio Mozzoni and to hunt here annually. The family line ended with Angela Mozzoni, who married Count Gian Pietro Cicogna in 1580; his descendants still own the property today.

Early in the sixteenth century, the Mozzoni brothers undertook a major renovation of the villa, and it remains largely in this form today. Frescoes have faded under portions of the three-sided, arcaded courtyard, but they have retained their charm, with trellis designs on the ceilings painted by the Campi brothers from Cremona. The piano nobile has an exceptional collection of antique furnishings and fresco decorations. This is one of the rare private houses open to the public in Italy. It is under the tutelage of the FAI (Fondo per l'Ambiente Italiano), but owned and very well maintained by the Counts Cicogna-Mozzoni.

The gardens begun by Ascanio Mozzoni were redesigned under Gian Pietro Cicogna. The formal gardens are built on narrow terraces; the property is on seven levels. To the south of the villa, adjacent to the courtyard, is a small sunken garden with formal box parterres and patches of lawn. A heavy chain smothered by ivy divides the garden from the courtyard. Two small rectangular fishponds with balustrades are built against the rusticated high west wall. This wall is decorated with statuary and empty plaque-frames beneath eighteenth-century busts, staggered in height to avoid monotony. Within the southern wall is a grotto. This is roofed over and forms a tiled terrace above, from which one can look down into the sunken garden and gain access to the upper long terrace, which lies parallel to the rear of the villa. Two graceful marble chalice fountains are set within the *tapis vert*. The upper sections of these date from the late sixteenth century; the lower basins are from a century later. In the center of the gar-

den is a large topiary dove nestled on a flower bed. Water jets lie hidden along the paths. The effect of the garden is predominately evergreen; the western wall is topped by an ilex hedge behind a balustrade, and in the sunken garden to the east, a tall ilex hedge covers the wall.

To the rear of the house is a long narrow terrace. Built into the hillside are two grotto-like arcades, with dripping water and abundant maidenhair fern, providing sheltered walks on sultry days—a typical Renaissance feature. At the north end of the house and adjacent to the former stable block is a second larger garden with small geometric-patterned beds and borders, a spacious lawn, and a lovely view of Lake Lugano. This garden is generally set aside for the exclusive use of the proprietors. Broad low steps link it to the courtyard rooms and to the long terrace above.

The most perfect feature of the garden is in the center of the long upper terrace: a water stair, flanked on either side by steep steps and rows of cypresses, descends from a small pavilion and ripples almost 150 feet down into a basin. The basin is level with the long windows in the salon, providing an exactly centered view of this cascade from inside the villa. Two graceful stone nymphs recline on either side of the Lion basin, so called because of its mask and paws. This water-stair is perfectly proportioned to the garden and more pleasing than the grander version at Lake Como's Villa d'Este.

The rest of the grounds form the residue of the hunting park, now landscaped in the English style with winding paths, clearings, occasional fountains, belvederes, and specimen trees. Two greenhouses are in full operation, one specializing in orchids.

Villa d'Este

Part of the splendor of the luxurious Grand Hotel Villa d'Este is its perfectly proportioned and orchestrated sixteenth-century cypress allée—a slender remnant of the former garden, but worthy of its fame.

The cardinal Tolomeo Gallio grew up at Cernobbio as a humble fisherboy. Returning here he chose Pellegrino Pellegrini to design him a villa, which was built between 1568 and 1615. Pellegrini was responsible for the cardinal's other residences, including Gravedona. Cardinal Gallio gathered around him the talented and famous men of his time, especially artists and writers. Villa d'Este saw periods of splendor, followed by long phases of neglect. At the cardinal's death in 1607, his nephew Tolomeo, duke of Vito, inherited the villa but did not choose to live there. He passed it on to the Jesuits at his death. They occupied the villa until 1769 when they began to rent out the property, first for a year to Count Marco Odescalchi, then in 1779 to General Marliani, who eventually purchased the villa and resided here for many years. The marquis Bartolommeo Calderara bought it for his wife, Vittoria Peluso, the famed ballerina "La Pelusina." She beautifully restored the damaged villa and park, reviving its dignity. Eugène Beauharnais (who was appointed viceroy of Italy by Napoleon) and his court stayed at the Villa d'Este as guests of the Calderaras. In tribute to his successful campaigns in Spain, and in the hope of luring him to remain at home, Countess Calderara built her second husband, the Napoleonic general Dominique Pirro, a series of mock fortifications on the hillside overlooking the garden. It is difficult, however, to imagine the general content to play war on Lake Como after his battles in Spain.

Caroline of Brunswick, the scandalous, estranged wife of England's heir apparent (in time, George IV), settled here in disgrace from 1815 until her death in 1821. Under her ownership the villa became famous, the interior redone in Empire style, the gardens anglicized. She built the first carriage road on the lake's edge, linking Moltrasio and Cernobbio, and created the present entrance to the villa. The villa was renamed Villa d'Este in honor of the Brunswicks' distant ancestor, Guelfo d'Este. With her lover, the courtier Bartolommeo Bergami promoted to High Chamberlain, she set up her own quixotic court and passed the final years of her vagabond life exiled from England.

After 1820 the villa was owned by the barons Ciani. In the fervor of Italy's unification, a costume ball was held in the gardens of Villa d'Este during the summer of 1861. Lovely women, dressed in local costumes decorated with emblems of their towns, sang and marched to patriotic music

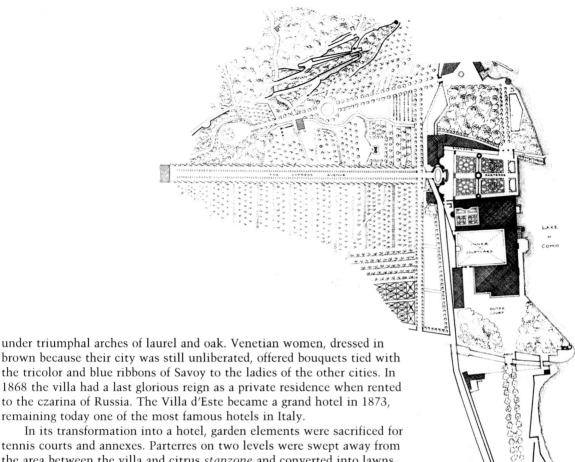

under triumphal arches of laurel and oak. Venetian women, dressed in brown because their city was still unliberated, offered bouquets tied with the tricolor and blue ribbons of Savoy to the ladies of the other cities. In 1868 the villa had a last glorious reign as a private residence when rented to the czarina of Russia. The Villa d'Este became a grand hotel in 1873, remaining today one of the most famous hotels in Italy.

In its transformation into a hotel, garden elements were sacrificed for tennis courts and annexes. Parterres on two levels were swept away from the area between the villa and citrus *stanzone* and converted into lawns. Fortunately the cypress allée and its imposing framing pavilions survived. The stucco and pebble-encrusted facades of the pavilions are picked out with designs of grotesques, pilasters, and niches set with vases. Obelisks and rounded pediments cap the roof line. These pavilions were designed to be mini-apartments for entertaining, but were never completed. Gentle steps rise to an oval court whose curving walls are decorated with caryatids and mythological bas-reliefs. In the center is a fishpond—a repository for the waters flowing from the *scalinate* (steps) above. Two rows of ancient cypresses line a grassy central path, flanked by the *scalinate*, which culminate at the top in a rebuilt Neoclassical temple with a large figure of the Italian poet Ariosto. Proportions are spacious and stately, Roman in feeling. Both Cardinal Gallio and Pellegrini traveled to Rome and Central Italy and were no doubt familiar with the water-stairs and twin pavilions of Caprarola. But Villa d'Este surpasses the Roman models in breadth and monumental dignity. This perspective is no doubt the work of Pellegrini, and dates from around 1570.

The pavilions divide the farm from the formal area of the garden adjacent to the villa. Beyond the cypress rows are open fields of olives and vineyards. Just behind the pavilion is a grindstone for crushing olives. Avenues of plane trees are laid out at a perpendicular angle to the cypress

Villa d'Este, from Triggs, *Art of Garden Design . . .* (1906).

allée, further setting apart the fields from the buildings. Following the avenue to the right, the allée turns into another avenue through a glen with English landscape plantings. A romantic ivy-covered bridge crosses a mountain torrent. Monte Brisbino looms behind the garden, heightening the sense of wilderness. The hillside is covered with a network of winding paths, flights of steps, waterfalls, and a fantastic assortment of small structures: old crumbling summerhouses, mock ruins, miniature forts—all relics of early nineteenth-century Romanticism. Walnut, acacia, and cypress trees grow over the hillside.

A grove of plane trees shades the marble-stepped water entrance. Beyond the *stanzone* is a small *bosco* leading to a clearing with a circular marble temple. This houses a statue of Minerva, goddess of wisdom and war, and a bust of Telemachus, son of Odysseus. Despite its transformations, the garden of Villa d'Este still evokes a sense of Baroque majesty.

41 · *Villa d'Este*

Villa Carlotta

*Cadenabbia, Lake Como
Gardens open to the public
from March to mid-
November*

Villa Carlotta draws crowds for its blazing display of color—150 varieties of rhododendrons and azaleas cover about fourteen acres in late May and June. For the botanist its vast collection of plants and trees from the far corners of the globe merits a visit. I have included it here less because of these undeniable attractions than for its original eighteenth-century portion. Villa Carlotta has one of the few gardens on Lake Como that maintain a disciplined Italian layout. Most lake gardens are less rigidly structured and tend towards the English landscape style because of their irregular shore lines and often steep terrain, plus the strong influence of the English expatriate colony in the lake district. The garden of Villa Carlotta spreads between Tremezzo and Cadenabbia. A sturdy, buff-colored, Neoclassical-style villa stands above a series of three broad descending terraces, allowing unimpeded views of Lake Como. Double stairways firmly link the levels, their sustaining walls covered with flowering vines. Bordering the villa are shrubs, flower beds, and palm trees. The second level consists of two trellised walks lined with oranges, lemons, and camellias—a shady scented retreat from the midday sun. The lowest terrace leads to the rounded fishpond set within towering, curved box hedges. A fountain of a winged cupid holding aloft a dolphin spouts a high jet of water. Lacey wrought-iron gates close off the main water approach with two sets of curved steps approaching the lake. These are on the main axis that passes through the center of the house to a grotto in the embankment wall behind. The gates are decorated with a gilded letter "C" topped with a coronet, for Carlotta. Statues cap the piers, and small *broderie* sections planted with begonias and little cone-shaped shrubs surround the graceful fishpond. The hedges are extensive, creating a *bosco*. Seen from the water, the white decorative balustrade zigzags alongside the green hedges. Statues of the four seasons top its piers. The waterfront undulates and is shaded by plane trees, making a pleasant promenade facing the peninsula of Bellagio. The Neoclassical Sommariva family chapel stands at the far left. The hills rise around the villa, with Monte Crocione to its rear and the emerald waters at its front—a gem-like setting for the villa and its garden terraces. The fine climate and sheltered location, the balance of man-made and natural elements all combine to make this garden justly famous.

The villa was built between 1690 and 1743 by an unknown architect for the extravagant marquis Giorgio Clerici to use as a summer home away from Milan. Marcantonio Dal Re's engravings show the villa recently completed with a smaller garden consisting of a terrace extending on both

sides of the villa to form *giardini segreti*, and terminating at either end with a pavilion. The area behind the villa featured a retaining wall cut out of the steep hillside with rusticated niches for statues and a grotto in late Baroque style. The front terracing and stairs remain the same today, except that the *bosco* of hedges now covers what originally was a delicate *broderie* parterre. Clerici was the president of the Lombardy Senate, a banker, and a grandee of Spain. At his death the villa was inherited by Claudia Clerici, who married Giovanni Battista Sommariva di Lodi in 1795. Sommariva scaled the social ladder from his start as a barber's assistant to become a lawyer, financier, and one of the Triumvirs of the Second Cisalpine Republic between 1800 and 1802. His rival, Francesco Melzi, vice-president of the Napoleonic Italian Republic of 1802 was at this time building his lavish Villa Melzi across the lake at Bellagio. Giovanni Battista Sommariva determined to surpass it in beauty. The park was enlarged considerably and the villa up-dated with Neoclassical stucco-work, a balustrade and clock added to its roof line. A temple to Friendship, described by Giacomo Bascape in 1835, had a gleaming metal roof and was perched on the garden's highest point, acting as a beacon across the lake. (This has not survived.)

In 1840, Sommariva's son sold the property to the Rubini family, but retained the Clerici chapel for his own family. Shortly thereafter, in 1842, the entire property was purchased by Princess Marianna, wife of Albrecht of Prussia. She in turn presented the villa to her daughter, Carlotta, at the time of her wedding to Prince George, duke of Saxe-Meiningen. Princess Carlotta had a taste for luxury and fine entertaining. A long ducal barge rowed by six liveried oarsmen dressed in white with green sashes and berets was kept ready by the water-steps to ferry passengers to parties and picnics. The Saxe-Meiningens devoted great attention to the gardens, enlarging them further by a romantic English garden complete with a "jungle" dell, banked with tree-ferns along a stream. Pleached alleys were replaced by lawns, planted with many kinds of palms, laurels, eucalyptus, papyrus, Japanese maples, myrtles, cork, banana trees, and cactus as well

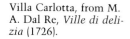

Villa Carlotta, from M. A. Dal Re, *Ville di delizia* (1726).

as clumps of pampas grass, bamboo, giant magnolias, a towering sequoia, Japanese *crytomeria*, and orchids from Brazil, the Himalayas, and Mexico. Fifteen kinds of *Clematis* thrive in the gardens today, along with over five hundred other varieties and species of plants, annuals, and bulbs. One section is devoted to a rock garden. The layout is much as the Saxe-Meiningens left it when the Italian government confiscated it as alien property at the beginning of World War I. Since 1927 the villa has been under the protection of the Ente Villa Carlotta, which maintains the gardens and the small museum with sculpture by Antonio Canova and Bertel Thorwaldsen, and paintings by Francesco Hayez.

While staying at Tremezzo Henry Wadsworth Longfellow wrote:

> By Sommariva's garden gate
> I make the marble stairs my seat
> And hear the water, as I wait,
> Lapping the stones beneath my feet.
>
> I ask myself, 'Is this a dream?
> Will it all vanish into air?
> Is there a land of such supreme
> And perfect beauty anywhere?'

(from Poems of Places, ed. H.W. Longfellow, 1877)

Villa Carlotta is still this beautiful today. Nightingales sing in the early morning, mixing their song with the splash of the fountain, the rustle of the foliage, and the lapping of the water.

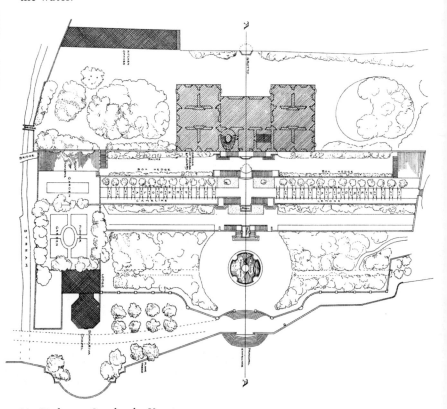

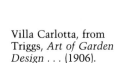

Villa Carlotta, from Triggs, *Art of Garden Design . . .* (1906).

Villa Crivelli

Inverigo
Gardens open (infrequently)
to the public

Above, right:
Villa Crivelli, watercolor
by J. C. Shepherd (1925).
British Architectural Li-
brary, R.I.B.A., London.

Villa Crivelli at Inverigo is in disastrous condition. However, its extraordinary garden concept can still be traced. The garden design consists of a series of cypress allées, which stretch for vast distances up the hillsides of the Piano d'Erba, connecting this villa with another, La Rotonda, designed by Luigi Cagnola for relatives of the Crivelli.

Inverigo is on the road from Bellagio to Milan. The Crivelli villa is set on a plateau, level with a small hamlet. By the parish church a gate leads to the villa, its entrance approach bordered by a relatively short cypress allée.

The Crivelli family owned this property continuously from the sixteenth century. Portions of the old castle including a *praetorium* and tower were incorporated into the late seventeenth-century villa. The castle was used during the Inquisitions; its prisons are still extant.

The villa's shape is irregular. It opens onto a series of three terraces, formerly parterres, bisected by the central allée. The remnants of the terrace garden have a set of four statues of Roman emperors facing the central path. The beds nearest the villa have been relegated to growing vegetables. The major portion of the terraces are now grassy slopes, cordoned off into a public park, infrequently open.

From the villa there are stupendous views of the valley and mountains beyond. Crossing a small road bordering the villa is the beginning of the majestic cypress allée, which descends the hillside and extends across the valley, interrupted by an entrance gate (unusual for Lombardy) at the main road, and then continues only to dissolve in a *bosco* beyond. The length of this spectacular allée is about one mile. It was never intended as a carriage drive as the slope is scaled by a series of steps—perhaps donkeys once navigated it.

The long cypress allée is on an axis with the garden terraces. After traversing them and another road on the plateau, the allée rises sharply up hill to a statue of Hercules, where it veers to the left along a ridge in the direction of La Rotonda.

In 1907 the marquis Crivelli made a serious attempt to restore the villa and its garden. For years the family discouraged visitors. But the villa has been uninhabited for the past thirty years and is now open to the elements, its once lavish parquet floors and frescoes are fast deteriorating. The last marquis Crivelli sold off parcels of adjacent land, which have been recently developed. The Villa Rotonda has fared better, it is now a home for the mutilated. It is to be hoped that the Villa Crivelli and its allées will be protected by the Belli Arte and eventually restored.

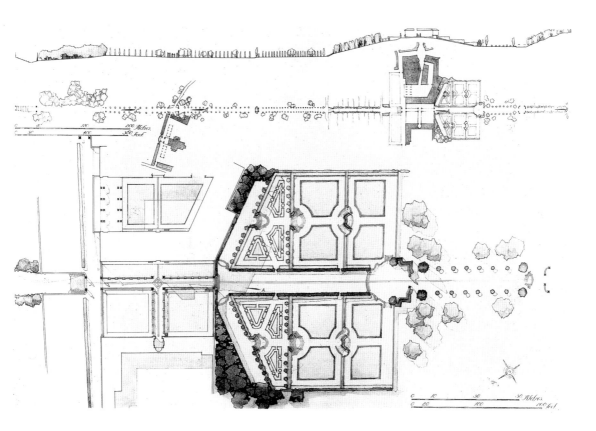

47 · Villa Crivelli

Villa Ducale

Colorno
Gardens open to the public

The fief of Colorno, long the property of the Sanseverino family, was confiscated by the dukes of Parma for many years. However, in 1580 it was returned to Barbara Sanseverino, embellished with a palace, by her elderly admirer, the duke Ottavio Farnese. But because of the political enmity between the duke and Barbara's father, the estate of Colorno was returned to her with the proviso that it would be inherited by Barbara's son, Girolamo.

A patroness of arts and letters, Barbara gathered painters and writers around her at the villa. (Correggio's famed *Marriage of Saint Catherine* and Raphael's *Portrait of Pope Leo X* as well as his *Madonna of the Cradle* were within the villa.) The Amorevoli, a literary academy consisting of Torquato Tasso, Muzio Manfredi, Giovanni Battista Guarini, and the duke Ottavio, met here.

Little is known about the garden of Barbara Sanseverino except that it was noted for its roses, and that Colorno, also called "La Rocca di Sanseverino," was more fortress than villa, bordered on one side by a torrent. Later it reverted back to the Farnese, who rebuilt it between 1660 and 1728 to a design of Ferdinando Galli-Bibiena for Ranuccio II and Francesco Farnese. It became a convenient summer residence within close reach of Parma.

In 1712 Francesco Farnese began to develop the garden, basing its design on the Grand Trianon of Mansart at Versailles. The Buffet du Trianon, a tiered fountain, was copied for Colorno in 1719. This stood off the main axis to the right, facing the garden facade. It was pulled down in 1883 and reinstalled in the piazza of the Reinach Theater in Parma a few years later. Subsequently it was moved to an island on the little lake at the end of the main viale of the Giardino Pubblico facing La Pilota, the Farnese palace.

Fountain of the Winds, Villa Ducale, from L. Dami, *Il Giardino Italiano* (1924).

The fountain is topped by two reclining ladies; between them water gushes out over three tiers below and three pedestal basins. This is the only remnant surviving the garden intact.

Originally the central axis led from the villa's staircase down a four part parterre of *broderie* design, flanked by four marble rusticated porticoes set with engaged columns. At the corners of the parterres, four cupids spouted jets of water across the path to the central fountain. A balustraded hedge with steps continued the axis and led into the second large area. Here were multiple low-edged parterres of *broderie*, statues, small round fountains, and lemon trees. At the end was a large round basin with the elaborate Fountain of the Winds. Tritons, hippocampi, and nereids on dolphins surrounded the central cup where the abduction of Persephone was represented. No trace of this remains today. The garden also featured a "magic" grotto, all covered with intricate mosaics, possibly originating from the Palatine hill in Rome.

The Villa Ducale in its day was famous for its garden. After 1815 the archduchess Marie Louise completely updated the garden in English landscape style. Between 1816 and 1820 the flat terrain was altered with brooks, artificial hills, woods, and clearings; the Fountain of the Winds was replaced by a lake. The garden suffered from bombardments in World War II, and the woods were cut down. Today efforts are being made to restore the villa; half the exterior has been freshly painted in yellow with white trim. The villa is massive, built around a central courtyard with four square towers at the corners. The park is open to the public and consists primarily of a large grassy clearing facing the monumental exterior staircase leading to the ducal apartments. Here a mossy mound marks the location of the first parterre fountain. The rest of the garden is a romantic woods, which encircles the small lake. The garden belongs to the town of Colorno.

Palazzo Doria

Genoa
Gardens open to the public

Genoa "the Proud" once had many stately gardens stretching from her waterfront up the hillsides, framing imposing palaces. These with very few exceptions have totally vanished due to land speculation and construction of roads and railroad tracks that slice through former gardens. It is a great pity, because the overall appearance of the crowded city suffers without these landscaped islands of green. It must have been spectacular as late as the eighteenth century to approach the city by water and see perched on the slopes gardens and villas such as Palazzo Doria.

Of all the Genoese gardens this was the most imposing. A portion of it remains today, but for the rest one must reconstruct in the mind's eye with the help of old descriptions and plans. In 1644 John Evelyn, the English diarist, wrote of the garden: "It reaches from the sea to the summit of the mountains" (*Diary*, ed. E. S. de Beer, 1959).

In 1521, as the inscription running across the outer wall of the palace states, Admiral Andrea Doria purchased villas belonging to the Lomellini and the Giustiniani as a site for his home, where he could "enjoy in peace the fruits of an honored life." At that time Genoa was involved with the French in a power struggle against Spain. The city was sacked by Spain's Imperial forces in 1528, and was on the verge of losing its freedom when Andrea Doria switched to the Spanish side, drove out the French, and negotiated a guaranteed independent Republic for Genoa. In September 1528 he proclaimed Carlo V of Spain the liberator. In turn, the emperor made him imperial admiral in the Mediterranean. Andrea Doria became the de facto head of the Genoese Republic, revising the constitution and strengthening the oligarchy; he was not to retire for many years. When Andrea Doria died at the age of ninety-five in 1560, the palazzo passed to his great nephew and heir, Giannandrea, who was also a naval commander in his own right.

Of the early Genoese palazzi this was the most important, conceived of more as a villa—facing the sea, airy and sunny. The main block by Caranca is irregular, somewhat disguised by a colonnade stretching its length and by two loggias designed by the Florentine Giovanni Angelo Montorsoli in 1529. Perino del Vaga, who fled Rome after the Spanish sacked the city in 1527, executed the frescoes in the Loggia of the Heroes, and also designed the pergola and terraces.

The gardens were divided into three parts: the first comprised the landing pier and lower parterre; the second was an irregularly shaped terrace with courtyards adjacent to the principal facade of the palazzo; the third, behind the house, consisted of a road to the entrance; a bridge over the road connected the palazzo with the upper garden extending up the hillside. Today this upper garden has disappeared.

Between 1539 and 1542 the grounds were transformed into gardens; additional land was given to Andrea Doria by the city of Genoa, which also moved a public road to insure his privacy. In 1540, to provide water for the fountains, the torrent of San Tommaso was shifted at great cost, and an aqueduct nearly one-half mile long was built. Huge cisterns were built into the hillside. The gardens took their final form between 1581 and 1599.

Two courtyards to the rear of the house frame small fountains. The north one built in 1577 is octagonal, with a putto riding a griffin atop a pedestal. The entrance courtyard has a more complex marble fountain of a monster, which Keysler writing around 1730 described as "the image of a monster, in its fore part resembling a satyr, with two little horns, but in the hind part it has a double fish's tail erect, and is said to have been taken alive" (G. S. Elgood, *Italian Gardens*, 1907). In 1581 Gian da Giacomo Valsoldo made this to replace an earlier fountain. It is surrounded by a marble balustrade with lobed corners, broken by steps on all four sides.

Loggias frame the center terrace with diamond-patterned pavement. Pebble ramps descend to the parterre garden. The garden covers an awkward terrain, with shifting levels and difficult angles; the parterre garden originally sloped, but was leveled in 1577. It was divided into six sections bordered by pergolas on the sides, with a large marble terrace and loggia overlooking the sea. In the center of the parterre is the large marble fish-

Palazzo Doria, from Triggs, *Art of Garden Design* . . . (1906).

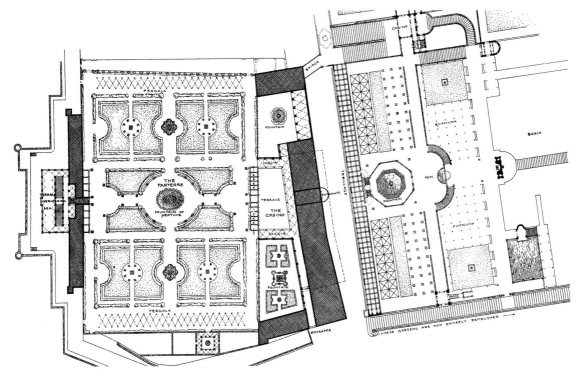

pond with a fountain of Neptune driving a team of seahorses, said to have been modeled in 1599 by the brothers Taddeo, Battista, and Giuseppe Carloni after Admiral Doria himself. The double-basin rim is ornamented with imperial eagles trampling serpents; baby tritons frolic in the water. In this lower garden there was an iron birdcage that enclosed large trees.

The marble terrace by the sea was the site of the famous banquet given for Carlo V at which three times the gold plate was cleared from the table and tossed into the sea below—needless to say, nets were carefully strung to receive it. Flights of steps beneath the terrace led to a grotto and direct access to the landing pier. In a sense this villa was also a naval base as Admiral Andrea Doria commanded twenty thousand men, soldiers, sailors, and slaves. Dungeons were built under the palazzo for his galley slaves.

Crossing the bridge one came to the largest area of the gardens, which was designed by Montorsoli. A pilastered and Doric-columned pergola matched the length of the palazzo's facade across the street. Large flower vases, portrayed in an engraving of about 1830 by Pierre Gauthier, were set on pedestals. Broad steps near the bridge led to an airy casino—a similar one was located further up the hill. On a higher level behind the pergola wall was a large raised octagonal fountain with surrounding balustrade, said to be of Captain Carcaro by Galeazzo Alessi. Triple rows of orange trees stood in tubs. The curving stairs led to the next level, which was planted with trees in *quincunx* pattern. A reservoir, later drained and used as a bowling alley, was located just beyond it. From here a central stair scaled the hillside, cutting through the ilex wood. At the summit an enormous niche was built in 1586 to house a colossal statue of Jupiter by the sculptor Marcello Sparti. The tomb of Roland, a favorite hound of Carlo V's, was just beneath it. The story goes that Andrea Doria was granted the principality of Melfi by the emperor, provided that Doria maintain the dog.

Pergola, Palazzo Doria, engraving by Pierre Gauthier (c. 1830).

Andrea Doria's nephew and heir, Prince Giannandrea Doria, destroyed the loggetta built in 1545 and transformed the palazzo once again in 1577 with the architect Giovanni Ponsello. He added service buildings and the loggia overlooking the sea, then the eastern loggia, the fishpond, Neptune Fountain, and the western loggia. The gardens took their final form between 1581 and 1599.

When the palazzo was inherited by Giannandrea II in 1627, it was no longer used as a main residence and a long decline began. The parterre design is now lost, having been replanted in 1844 with trees and shrubs blocking the view, but the three fountains remain, as does the huge Jupiter on the hillside. The palace was transformed from residence to hotel to office buildings. The upper gardens were gradually built over early in this century. The Palazzo Doria is located directly behind Genoa's main railroad station. Tracks now pass across the upper gardens, and the sea front is covered with city docks and warehouses. From the Via Adua one can get a glimpse of what once was Genoa's noblest garden.

At present the rear facade of the Palazzo Doria is undergoing major restoration. A handsome building of stucco adorned with loggias, white marble balustrades, and portals—it certainly merits this renewal. I hope that the facing garden will also be deemed worthy of maintaining; now it is a sad testimony to neglect. The fountains are dry and sit isolated among weeds. The lobed fountain near the entrance does still have its box hedges, but its rocky mount with Triton stands in an empty basin. A congregation of stray cats is clustered nearby. In the lower level, the area has been blocked off to create a summer open-air cinema. The Neptune Fountain stands beyond the rows of seats amid uncut grass.

Much of the original impact of the garden generated from its seaside site, now totally obscured by an overpass with cars whizzing by and the rambling Stazione Marittima by the docks. However, the bare bones of the loggiaed palazzo, its terraces, fountains, and pebble paths survive, and should be displayed properly. The garden as it exists now in a reduced scale requires minimal maintenance, and for historic reasons—this was Genoa's most famous garden, and is the last survivor of its kind—it deserves to be conserved and enjoyed.

53 · *Palazzo Doria*

Villa Cuzzano

Cuzzano
Gardens open occasionally
for banquets and con-
ferences, but visitors
are not encouraged

Villa Cuzzano deserves notice as a typical seventeenth-century garden of the Veneto, remarkably intact. The actual area covered by the garden is small, but it "borrows" the space of its surrounding valley through simple, yet carefully thought-out measures, and the resulting impression is of vast scale. The concept of extended or "borrowed" space beyond the garden proper was typical of the Veneto. Unfortunately, since the majority of these gardens were laid out on plains, they were much more vulnerable to change than the stone terracing and steps of hillside gardens, and few remain in their original form.

Around 1300 the property belonged to the dal Verme family, then to the Dandolo, followed by the Turisenda Alcenago family. By 1500 the Allegri were in possession. This family held a monopoly on all olive production and animal slaughtering in the Valpatena. In 1653 there were 260 fields, reduced to 194 by 1745. The Allegri sold the property in 1824 to Giovanni Antonio Arvedi of Verona. He had three sons: one an engineer, another a silk manufacturer in Verona, the third a passionate hunter who died in a fall from his horse while only in his twenties. Their sister, Lucidalba, took holy vows and founded her own order, the Arvediane, housing the nuns in another family villa at Poiano. (When the order was reduced to five members it was absorbed by the Canossione.) Lucidalba is responsible for the courtyard's empty niches. Offended by the pagan subject matter of the statues in the niches and atop the balustrade, she ordered the sculptures to be thrown in the nearby riverbed, and had a fresco in the villa by Paolo Veronese destroyed. In the next generation Pietro Arvedi, a patriot, fully supported the Irredentist movement to annex to Italy the Italian territories under Austrian control, landing him in prison in Austria for twenty years.

The villa can be seen clearly from the roadside, majestically set on a terrace at the foot of the hill. It was built by 1650 (the completion date for the frescoes) for Giovanni Battista Allegri di Gerolamo by the architect Giovanni Battista Bianchi. In the nineteenth century Giovanni Antonio Arvedi had intended to rebuild the villa, but fortunately left it as it was. It sprawls comfortably across the width of the garden, set on a grassy terrace, with a wide first-floor balcony overlooking the parterre. Older square towers anchor the wings and statues line its rooftop. To the rear, a spacious courtyard separates the villa from the chapel. The Allegri built this commemorative chapel in honor of San Carlo Borromeo's halt here en route to the Council of Trent. This raised, elegant chapel is one of the few in pri-

55 · *Villa Cuzzano*

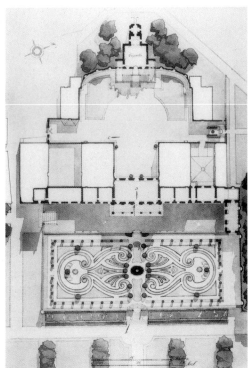

vate hands where mass is still celebrated on a regular basis. Inside the courtyard to the right, a pair of steps around a central niche with a statue leads to an informal garden on a higher elevation, framed by cypresses. Standing within the raised chapel one looks on a direct axis across the courtyard, through the central salon of the villa, and out the front door to the *broderied*-parterre terrace placed below the villa, and still beyond to the surrounding hills. The *broderie* is in the French seventeenth-century taste and consists of large arabesques in low box, in keeping with the sense of spaciousness of the surrounding cultivated fields and rolling hills. There are no angular lines here. The yews are clipped in soft rounded forms for punctuation, and an oval pool centers the design. The rose bushes and peonies add color. The eye is led via sets of large statues and gently curving rows of yews to a sloping entrance road bordered by hedges, beyond which majestic cypresses mark the end of the garden. The original approach road was straight, leading to the villa's terrace, subsequently a curve and new entrance pavilion were introduced.

Oil, wine, and honey are still produced on the land. Next to the villa is housed the press, which crushes the olives growing on a third of the property today. Beehives are lined up against a wall covered with caper vines. Pet dogs and three strutting peacocks wander through the garden. It is loveliest before Easter when the Judas tree in the courtyard is in red-violet bloom, or in September/October when the mellow walls are aflame with Virginia creeper. Magnolia, cypress, khaki, oleander, forsythia, chestnut, and camphora also grow in the gardens. The villa is now the home of Ottavio Arvedi and his family.

Villa Rizzardi

Negrar
Gardens open to the public

Spread over a hillside in the Valpolicella is the eighteenth-century garden of Villa Rizzardi. This was one of the last classical Italian gardens to be made in Italy, and it remains quite unchanged.

Luigi Trezza designed this garden over a period of years, beginning in 1783. Its owners, the counts Rizzardi, knew that an ancient Roman pleasure garden had covered a portion of the valley, including their property. Using this historical precedent, they designed the garden to recreate in spirit a Roman classical garden with a strong axial plan linking the house and garden, and an open-air theater. Count Rizzardi was a trader from Verona; his wife was English. They wanted portions of the garden to recall places where they had formerly lived—Greece, England, and India. Aided by their business contacts, they imported plants from these countries as well as from Japan and China. Early in the 1800s their greenhouse attracted visitors to view rarities extinct elsewhere.

The villa itself was rebuilt in the second half of the nineteenth century, and is now occupied by the Spanish sculptor Miguel Berrocal. Further up the road is the gardener's lodge and entrance used for visitors to the garden.

The rear of the house faces a small private garden with fountains and box borders. Lemon trees mark the beginning of an allée of clipped elms, their upper branches almost touching in the center. Irises grow along the edges. This shady allée is the first of a series, each different in character, which link the garden on varying levels. The elm allée terminates with four large cypresses framing a leafy niche with statues.

Turning right is the second allée, this of cypress, marching up the sloping hillside to a belvedere. Proceeding up this allée one comes shortly to the entrance of the green theater on the left, marked by stone lions. This is the last and largest of a series of important green theaters built in Italy. Trezza and his clients searched a number of years for the ideal location, finally settling on this. The acoustics are perfect. In the Biblioteca Civica of Verona there is a plan by Trezza of this theater dated 1796. It is Greek in inspiration, severe in design, consisting of seven tiers cut against the hillside. Each of the turf seats is edged with clipped box and topped with statues by Pietro Muttoni. The stage is ample, with hedge wings; it even has a round green changing room off to the right.

Midway up the hillside the allée branches off to the right and marches across the meadow. The cypresses are interspersed with Spanish dagger. At certain times of the year the flowers creating a swath of color on this field

59 · *Villa Rizzardi*

can be seen from the village below—in autumn, the hillside is covered with blooming crocuses.

The belvedere is graceful, with pretty steps leading to a lookout shared with stone putti. In the past, musicians played atop the structure while guests sipped tea below.

Turning to the right, one enters a *bosco* that once had centuries-old oak, cut down during the Austrian occupation of the Veneto. A star-shaped path led past statues of wild beasts. In the middle of the *bosco* is a circular mock ruin, open to the sky, with niches of *spugne.* This was intended as a cool dining retreat.

Coming out of the woods, one passes a grove of palms, and then on the highest level of the garden enters a small viale of hornbeam, where in late January the first flowers, amoretti and narcissus, appear. For eleven months there will be continual flowering in the garden.

The path turns to the right and descends among flower beds to a small, circular lemon garden with a round fishpond in its center.

Next to the house is a secret garden, hidden by hedges from the rest of the garden. It is reached by a bridge from the first story of the villa and is built on two levels. Here beds are planted with rose bushes, and fountains are set into the retaining walls. In the upper level water plays over a huge stalactite.

The late count Rizzardi had serious plans to restore the garden to perfection. He opened it to the public, so that the villagers of Negrar could enjoy the fruits of their ancestors' labors. He died in 1984, but his widow continues to allow access to the garden. When I saw it they had been without a chief gardener for some time, and the countess Rizzardi no longer lived on the premises. It is hoped that the garden will continue to be maintained and opened to the public, because it is of exceptional interest for its design and its lovely site, with views from all parts of the garden.

Giardini Giusti

Verona
Gardens open to the public
(apply at palace for entry)

Little is known about the formation of the Giardini Giusti of Verona—no early plans, documents, or engravings exist to guide us through its transformations. However, there are written accounts of many illustrious visitors of the seventeenth and eighteenth centuries. Goethe in 1786 was so entranced by the garden that he carried off branches of its monstrous cypress as a bouquet, astonishing the Veronese he passed in the streets.

The Giusti family came to Verona from Tuscany in the fifteenth century. Their complete name, Giusti del Giardino, implies that the family early on was unique in Verona for possessing a real garden as opposed to a vegetable garden, vineyard, or orchard. The garden layout, more Tuscan in spirit than of the Veneto, incorporates the terraced hillside, but of the original design only the grand cypress allée remains. The earliest written account of the garden is from 1608 by the Englishman Thomas Coryat who describes the thirty-three cypresses, a shell-decorated grotto, the terraced hilltop with pavilion for refreshment, fountains, and parterres. Georgina Masson dates the garden before 1570 from the existence of Cyprian shells, which would have been unobtainable after that date because of Turkish rule.

After a day's sightseeing in the narrow streets of Verona, it is a relief to cross the river to the Giardini Giusti. An archway leads into a courtyard and a large grilled gate sets off the garden beyond. The ancient cypress allée lines the path to this gate, leading across the shallow, level garden to the hill of San Zeno in Monte. The allée scales San Zeno straight up to a level, where it splits off at right and left angles across the crest of the hill; woods back the cypresses. I love this garden on an autumn afternoon, when the piano music of the ballet school in a wing of the palazzo filters through across the shadows of the garden.

John Evelyn's diary from 1644 reads, "At the entrance of this garden grows the goodliest cypress I fancy, in Europe, cut in a pyramid" (*Diary*, ed. E. S. de Beer, 1959). This tree survived seven hundred years, and died only early in this century. Charles de Brosses describes the cypresses throughout the garden as being prodigiously high and pointed, giving an air to the garden as suitable for a location to hold a witches' sabbath.

In 1732 the Italian dramatist and scholar Marquis di Maffei described a fishpond encircled by a balustrade and an island in the center adorned with a statue by Alessandro Vittoria. No trace of this survives.

The garden always featured a maze. In his *L'Italie il y a cent ans* (1858) de Brosses describes getting caught in it: "J'y fus une heure au grand

soleil à tempêter, sans pouvoir me retrouver, jusqu'à ce que les gens de la maison vinssent m'en tirer." The maze was redesigned in 1786 by Luigi Trezza, but it disappeared early in this century. Charles Adams Platt speaks in his book, *Italian Gardens* (1894), of the garden's deplorable state—much overgrown, fountains filled in, and the overall view of the parterres blocked from a height by the tall trees within the garden. Happily the gardens are now well maintained.

The great masks carved out of the rock that supports the terrace balcony are still there. The terraces command sweeping views of the city, the Tyrol Alps, and Mantua far in the distance. The top terrace has a graceful little pavilion, possibly reconstructed in the nineteenth century. A spiral stair leads up to the highest level with an even loftier view.

Antique pedestals and many of the original statues are gone; those remaining, mostly of maidens in swirling drapery, are charming. The lower flat level of the garden is divided by the cypress allée. To the left are low clipped box hedges enclosing a flower garden with potted lemon trees. A dense wall of shrubs and evergreens hides the hillside. These were probably planted in the nineteenth century when the English garden craze took over. To the right of the allée is a grove of trees and the new maze. Here and there are simple fountains and graceful statues.

The garden is open to the public and rarely crowded on a weekday.

> Verona, thy tall gardens stand erect,
> Beckoning me upward. Let me rest awhile
> Where the birds whistle hidden in the boughs.
>
> Walter Savage Landor, c. 1860

Villa la Deliziosa

Montegaldella
Gardens open to the public
Thursday and Saturday
mornings

Villa la Deliziosa, formerly Villa Conti, is noteworthy for its lively population of eighteenth-century statuary by Orazio Marinali, its seventeenth-century embracing walls, and the gates that pierce them. The garden plan itself, however, is unimaginative.

Pietro Conti had the villa and garden designed in 1622. His family held extensive land in the area until the nineteenth century when both the villa and gardens were greatly changed. Basically it consists of a simple three-story block with a four-columned portico. Six statues are silhouetted against the sky on the rooftop. They were probably part of the original villa design. The chapel built in 1741 is dedicated to Santa Eurosia and Santa Irene. Connected to the villa is a long three-sided, deep portico. This shady walkway once contained stables and farm storage but today houses a caretaker and his family—the clucking of chickens is still heard within its walls. At one end, a grilled gate opens onto the fields beyond; another gate is found at the far right corner opening onto the street. This portico surrounds the front garden, broken only by the two sets of tall entrance gates topped with statues. The front garden is now informally planted with a large beech tree, two magnolias facing the villa, hydrangeas, and two rose beds.

The more interesting portion of the garden is found to the rear of the villa. Here a park is divided by straight paths regularly studded with statues from the shop of Marinali. The figures depicting the eighteenth-century Commedia dell'Arte are especially fine. Goddesses surround the rose

bed. A towering sculptural group, called La Ruota was designed by Marinali to represent the four corners of the world as reclining river gods, with Jupiter and another male figure above three standing female figures. Putti straddle the volutes. Originally the gardens contained 164 statues of which about fifty remain including those on the gateways and rooftops. Marinali also produced statues for Villa Trissino near Vicenza. The sets of gates leading from the street to this rear garden are the most beautiful, the iron-work is of lacy fleur-de-lis, and four statues crown its columns, now over-grown with ivy.

The villa is on the main road of Montegaldella. Opposite the *comune*, or town hall, and the road weighing station is a tawny wall with three extraordinary gates, then a family chapel, and another gate. It is useless to ring doorbells on the street side. If it is a Thursday or Saturday morning it is possible to visit the gardens ignoring the gateways facing the road. Just beyond the chapel an unmarked dirt road, or more properly, a track, leads through a field bordering the villa's walls. At the far corner of the wall, turn left along a hedge to the tall impressive entrance gate. If it is not a day when the villa is open you must content yourself with peering through the exquisite wrought-iron gates. The villa is now the property of the town of Montegaldella.

Villa Barbarigo

Valsanzibio
Gardens open to the public
daily from mid-March
to mid-November (closed
Monday mornings)

Villa Barbarigo, also called Villa Donà dalle Rose, is tucked away in the valley of Valsanzibio, formed by the Euganean hills four miles from Battaglia. A rarity among seventeenth-century gardens of the Veneto, it has survived, probably because of the unusual use of its site. The cross-plan is disarmingly simple, the long axis stretches across the valley and up the sides of the hills. This is clearly defined by an allée of cypresses rising sharply up Monte Berici behind the unpretentious villa, continuing in front with a piazzale and then by an allée bordered by impressive beech hedges, ending in broad grassy steps up the opposite hill. Fountains, statues, and large lemon pots punctuate this allée. At the center, a transverse axis slopes gently, carrying water down gradually from level to level, ending in a pool before the water-gate. In former days, the Veneto was criss-

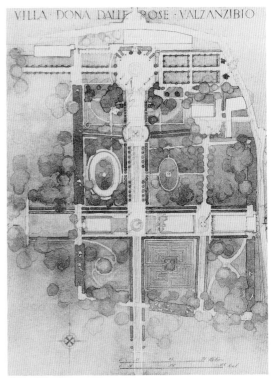

crossed by canals, convenient waterways for travel between Padua and Venice. The gateway, a remnant from that era, is constructed to frame a view of the cascade for the passersby—a feature much found in France but rarely in Italy.

The property belonged first to the Michiel family, and in turn to the Martinengo in the sixteenth century, the Barbarigo in the seventeenth century, followed by the Donà dalle Rose, the Segré, and presently by the Pizzoni Ardemani family.

The original garden plan dates from 1669, when it was owned by the procurator of San Marco of Venice, Antonio Barbarigo. Certain formal areas were subsequently transformed into woods in the Romantic period, parterres and evergreens replaced with deciduous trees such as elms and planes. World War II brought general neglect and the destruction of many of the trees. But now, thanks to replanting and conscientious upkeep the gardens are again lovely. In fact in places, the towering vegetation is so lush that it obscures an appreciation of the garden's features. The overall impression of the garden is one of restrained Baroque.

As is typical of Veneto gardens, the surrounding vistas count heavily in the general effect. Hillsides remain in their natural state, not tamed into terraces as in the gardens of Tuscany and Rome.

The two-story, vine-covered villa is a simple block, set on a terrace facing across the valley. Behind the villa is a small semicircle of rusticated niched walls, topped with a balustrade, and bisected by broad steps ascending the base of the mountain. A double row of two-hundred-year-old cypresses marches up the steep slope into wilderness—a very Baroque touch. The circular piazzale facing the villa was probably once a parterre area. The round fountains and steps are riddled with trick jets, which still function. Statues set on pedestals inscribed poetically watch over the piazzale.

To one side of the long allée is the complex labyrinth, with a columned loggia on a raised platform in its center. The labyrinth was replanted after World War II. On the opposite side of the allée an island with a domed aviary floats on a formal round pond. Stone rabbits stand on the

Left:
Villa Barbarigo, watercolor by J. C. Shepherd (1925). British Architectural Library, R.I.B.A., London.

Above, right:
Rabbit Island, Villa Barbarigo, engraving by Vincenzo Campana (18th century).

balustraded outer edge of the pond. This was the rabbit island, a not uncommon feature in gardens of the past, dating back to Roman Imperial times as the *leporarium*. A charming early eighteenth-century engraving by Vincenzo Campana depicts this island teeming with frolicking rabbits.

The water-gate forms a rusticated triumphal arch with a broken pediment. Its theme is Diana's Bath. The roof line is adorned with statues of the hunters: Diana, Actaeon, and Endymion, with stags and dogs. In niches are bas-reliefs of trophies, and statues of peasants emptying casks into the basin, which is all that remains of the canal originally running along the main road. Access to the garden is through hidden small doors on the sides. Through the archway is a view of the transverse axis interspersed with fountains, statuary, and stretches of lawn gently descending to the water-gate.

At the opposite end of the allée the valley closes with wooded hills. Reclining nereids and tritons blowing conch shells mark two cascades. Water flows from the hills of Gallodona via tubes to the canals and basins. One low polygonal basin, the so-called Flowers Fountain, has a standing putto supporting a basket of fruit and flowers upon his head. From this, jets of water shoot out in different patterns over the pebbled surface of the pool. At the junction point of the two allées is a charming low, round fountain with seated putti on its rim, dangling their feet in the water.

A tunnel of hornbeam is off the main allée. Hedges of clipped box lead to the house. A treatise on plants in 1726 by Paolo Bartolommeo Clarici, *Istoria e cultura delle piante*, made special note of the hardy and unusually large double stocks that were grown in this garden.

A hermitage deep in the thick woods, a green theater with side wings of hedges, and a huge, winged statue of Father Time being crushed by age, are some of the other features of the garden. Among the old engravings of it, one shows a lemon avenue with columned pergola and fountain. Trick jets spring from the sides of the path and along the steps leading to the pergola.

Villa Pisani

Stra
Gardens open to the public
(closed Mondays)

Among the many ghost-like villas that line the Brenta canal looms Villa Pisani at Stra, surpassing all others in scale and lavishness. Truly, it is more palace than villa with its stately edifices and vast park. It must be said that its garden concept is eighteenth-century French, but it is included here as a re-importation, since the germ of French gardening derived ultimately from Italy. Its elaborate *broderie* parterres vanished when the gardens underwent radical transformations in the nineteenth century, but the straight allées, which cut through the woods to end at pierced garden gates set in the encircling garden walls, and the recently built canal, which provides a sheet of water as opposed to rippling Italian cascades, are both very French features.

The Pisani family had an earlier sixteenth-century villa on this site which Doge Alvise Pisani decided to replace around 1730. The park of almost twenty-five miles was already well underway by 1728; Girolamo Frigimelica, a Paduan noble, designed its maze, an archway with six openings, and a belvedere. Pisani then commissioned Frigimelica to design a palace, the model of which is kept at the Museo Correr. Frigimelica's designs for the stables and garden pavilions were carried out, but interruptions, which removed him to Modena slowed the progress of the palace. At his death in 1732 the project was handed over to Francesco Maria Preti, who modified the design substantially, especially the facade in Neo-Palladian style, completing it by 1740.

Alvise Pisani loved ostentation and pomp, and as a diplomat was said to have traveled with an entourage of all the Venetian royalty. He represented Venice in France where Louis XIV became godfather to his son, and also served in England. Upon his return to Venice in 1735 he was elected doge. Besides building Villa Pisani, he spent lavishly on his Venetian family palazzo in Piazza Santo Stefano.

Villa Pisani hosted distinguished guests, among them the children of Catherine the Great of Russia, Archduchess Maria Elisabetta of Austria, and King Gustav III of Sweden. Although the male line died out around 1750, the Pisani family held the property until 1807 when it was sold to Napoleon. He and Josephine had admired it in 1797, but after purchasing it, slept there only one night in November 1807 en route from Padua to Venice. He soon gave it to Eugène Beauharnais, viceroy of Italy, who renamed it Villa Eugenia. Carlo IV, the deposed king of Spain, came to stay for two months in 1817, with his wife Marie Louise of Parma, her lover Manuel de Godroy, and their entourage of one hundred people. They de-

Labyrinth, Villa Pisani, engraving by G. B. Carboni and N. Randonnette.

stroyed the wall coverings and rugs by waxing them, perhaps to make them look like leather. Subsequently, Archduke Maximilian stayed here. When the Veneto was incorporated into the Kingdom of Italy the property became state owned. Villa Pisani was the meeting place of Hitler and Mussolini in 1943. In recent years the palace has been restored, its gardens tidied up and opened to the public.

The palazzo faces the road, its gardens stretching out behind with woods to the sides. At various points in the enclosing high wall are handsome gates with wrought-iron grills. From these gates long transverse allées cut across the park, meeting in the central allée that crosses the garden. The gates thus provide *claires-voies*—long vistas to be enjoyed from the exterior of the garden. The water-gates along the curving Brenta are particularly elegant. The principle one is a triumphal arch topped by a terrace and a dainty temple. Access to it is provided by spiral staircases, which encircle two flanking Corinthian columns. Behind the palace, set in a long, wide lawn between rows of trees, is a long canal ending in a lobed basin with curving steps descending to a balustrade. This was added at the end of the last century when the palazzo was used as an engineering school, and the canal built for hydraulic experiments. The canal visually links the palace with the stables that face it; the result is surprisingly harmonious and adds to the stateliness.

Frigimelica's white- and peach-colored stables are splendid, porticoed, turreted structures with rounded ends that serve as orangeries. The stables have twenty-four stalls, marked with red marble posts, each surmounted by a golden statuette of a horse in a different pose.

Statues are everywhere, studding the canal, adorning high pedestals, and populating the roof lines. Many more were carried off to France under Napoleon, others vanished to Austria under Emperor Francis I. Except for those by Giovanni Francesco Bonazza, most are by unknown sculptors.

Scattered within the park are small romantic constructions left over from the formal garden. Set in the middle of a maze is a small circular tower, with a spiral staircase entwined around its outer walls. At a junction of paths is an elegant hexagonal archway with arbors stretching off on two sides; a stairway hidden in a pilaster of the archway leads to the rooftop. Tucked away in the woods is a mount, with broad steps leading to a breezy pavilion, once surrounded by a moat. Because the terrain is flat, these belvedere constructions were favored. The effect is lost today, as tall elms and lime trees crowd around them, and the flower beds whose pat-

terns could be enjoyed from above, are gone.

Because of the numerous deciduous trees it is advisable to visit the park in the autumn when the leaves are golden and scattered over the green lawns—a melancholy season suiting the vast emptiness of Villa Pisani. It is a lonely, haunted garden, the trees whispering of former grander times, of gaiety and intrigue. It touched the poet Gabriele D'Annunzio, who used it as the setting for his autobiographical novel *Il Fuoco*. The hero Stelio Effrena comes here with his mistress, the great actress, La Foscarina (in real life D'Annunzio's love, Eleanora Duse). They tour the overpowering vacant palace, then lose themselves in the gardens. He describes the statues (trans. K. Vivaria, 1900):

> "They were countless, a scattered population, still white or grey, or yellow with lichens, or greenish with moss, or spotted, in all poses, in all gestures. Gods, heroes, nymphs, seasons, hours, with bows, arrows, garlands, cornucopias, torches, and all the emblems of power, wealth and voluptuousness, exiled from fountains, grottos, labyrinths, pergolas, porticoes, friends of box and myrtle, evergreens, protectors of fleeting loves, and witnesses to eternal oaths, figures of a dream much older than the hands which formed them, and of eyes which had contemplated them in destroyed gardens."

II *Tuscany*
Marche

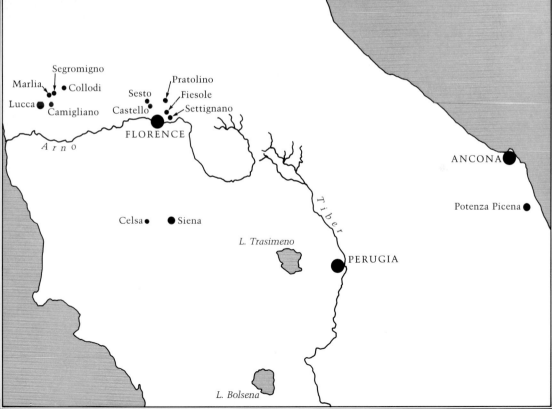

Segromigno

Marlia

Collodi

Lucca

Camigliano

Sesto

Pratolino

Fiesole

Castello

Settignano

FLORENCE

Arno

ANCONA

Celsa

Siena

Potenza Picena

L. Trasimeno

Tiber

PERUGIA

L. Bolsena

76 · *Tuscany, Marche*

Villa Torrigiani

Camigliano
Gardens open to the public
(closed Thursdays)

Most gardens in the Lucchese countryside have been transformed into the English landscape style. Villa Torrigiani did not completely escape this fashion, but happily preserves its seventeenth-century sunken secret garden.

Villa Torrigiani is near the village of Camigliano, only a mile from the Villa Mansi. A stately cypress allée in line with the main axis of the villa stretches one-half mile to a cluster of housing built for the garden staff. The allée is perpendicular to a lane punctuated by mock mini-defensive turrets leading to the family chapel and campanile.

The first mention of the villa is made in a trial record of 1593, regarding the assassination of Lelio Buonvisi, whose family owned the property at the time. The Santini family rebuilt the villa in the second quarter of the seventeenth century, transforming the southern facade facing the valley. In 1816 Vittoria Santini married Pietro Guadagni, the marquis Torrigiani, whose descendant, Princess Colonna Torrigiani, owns the villa today. In effect, a Mannerist front was applied to the building, creating contrasts of smooth stucco and rough stonework. It has been suggested that the architect was Muzio Oddi. A fan-shaped staircase leads to a Serlian portico entry which is repeated in rusticated pilasters above. Balustrades dotted with statuary emphasize the three stories of the facade. On top, a square attic with a terrace served as a theater. The result is a rather heavy piece of confectionary set among large trees and grassy lawns with two multi-edged fountain pools in front of the villa. Just beyond the gate are remnants of a once formal parterre area with *broderied*, quadri-partite areas and potted citrus, all bordered by hedges. The earlier garden plan was executed in the second half of the seventeenth century for the Santini family in the French style. At this time the immediate open area around the villa was set off from the lower parterres by a low wall with urns, statuary, and a short flight of steps. A slight rise in the lawn recalls this. Similarly, to the rear of the villa was a large round fountain basin with four parterre sections and a hedge cut with niches for statuary; beyond a small gate, as today, spread the family vineyards. The round pool remains, surrounded by uncut grass. Otherwise the area so far described was altered by Vittoria Santini to meet the nineteenth-century taste *à l'anglaise,* with open lawns countered by bushes and trees to achieve a natural effect. To the rear on the left, paths descend into a shady *bosco.* The Torrigiani family have an eighteenth-century engraving of the original garden plan, as well as a design by G. F. Farnocchia dating from 1797 in which the parterre designs are a bit stiffer, and the flower beds are grouped differently in the sunken hidden garden. One other feature of the garden has been lost with time—to the rear of the house at the right was a small allée of trees. This had symmetrical niches on either side, filled with statuary and fountains. Only a winged figure of Saturn, the god of agriculture, remains at the end on the right. This allée led to one side of the long rectangular fishpond, bordered by potted citrus and cypresses, which reflect in the pool. A delightful marble siren surveys the pond.

The fishpond forms part of a terrace, which is bordered by the flight of steps at its foot, descending down into the secret garden of Flora. In the past there was a high wall here with porthole openings, enhancing the element of surprise, which the garden offers below. A pretty rectangular area of flower beds grouped around two small round fountains continues towards a hemicycle wall with a cupola topped grotto at the far end. The sunken garden was designed on a straight axis, culminating at the stone grotto. Within the octagonal-shaped grotto are charming marble figures representing the winds, set against rough stalactites and niches of alternating smooth and rough materials. There are pebble mosaics in the arches and cornices, pilasters at the corners, and a black- and white-pebble pavement in spiral pattern. This garden has a complete series of *giochi d'acqua*, or water jets, which attack from all directions. A water curtain cuts off one's exit from the grotto. If you escape to the flanking staircase leading to the belvedere terrace and cupola, the water jets pursue you. The tile-covered cupola is crowned by a statue of Flora poised on top of volutes supported by masks. Wrought-iron flowers surround her feet and fill a basket on her head. Water springs from these flowers in a chandelier effect. The secret garden's parterre pattern, after being abandoned in the 1920s, has been restored to the earlier of the eighteenth-century designs.

Within the entry staircase is a subterranean passageway connecting the villa to the secret garden. Just outside the garden is an attractive casino with an attached lemon house, which is entered by a small parterred rose garden with raised flower borders. A parterre area also exists adjacent to the house, but is not linked to it and lacks the unity of the walled gardens. The area to the left of the villa has always been reserved as a wilderness for game and birds.

Villa Torrigiani is best seen in the autumn when the Virginia creeper turns red, and the salvia in the beds contrasts with its green box borders.

Villa Mansi

Villa Mansi at Segromigno was a Baroque garden partially transformed into an English landscape garden. As a result we are left with Baroque fragments by Filippo Juvarra, surrounded by a spacious lawn and stately trees. The villa facade—Renaissance with Mannerist overlays—dominates the garden.

We know that a former villa on the site was originally owned by the Benedetti family, who sold it in 1599 to the Cenami. Between 1634 and 1635 Countess Felice Cenami hired Muzio Oddi of Urbino to build a new villa. Letters survive from her brother-in-law in Paris, Abbot Paolo Cenami, who followed and advised on the construction in minute detail. This villa was rectangular with two slightly projecting wings, and a loggia flush with the central block reached from the exterior by two ramp staircases. Ottavio Mansi acquired the villa in 1675, and received the future Frederick IV of Denmark here. In 1742, another abbot, Giovan Francesco Giusti, acting as architect, raised the central facade a story, and added balustrades, statues, and the Mansi name and arms. He left us elevations of the front facade, as well as six views and two plans of the villa and garden from which were made a set of engravings. Juvarra designed various gardens in the Lucca area, but this appears to be the only one carried out between 1725 and 1732. For Ottavio Mansi, Juvarra divided the garden enclosure into unsymmetrical sections. The formal areas were placed to the south of the villa; a lawn, bisected by the approach drive, separated them.

At the bottom left of the garden was an elaborate tri-partite garden; a curving basin followed by a parterre of arabesques led to a *vialetto* of potted citrus and flower beds, ending at a round fountain surrounded by undulating hedges. This garden was planned optically to appear larger; the parterre of a trapezoidal form and the curving hedges aided the illusion. The section was destroyed as it was considered too formal when the garden was redone in the nineteenth century in the English mode.

The approach to Villa Mansi is by a public road perpendicular to the surrounding lane. The entrance gate is marked by a small semicircular esplanade, from here the main garden road crosses two successive areas on different levels to emerge in the quadrangular court of the villa. The garden gradually reveals itself as you explore it. Like Marlia, the villa today lacks a central viale.

Juvarra aimed at varied effects in this garden. Facing the villa on your right are the remains of his *bosco*, a shady woods once traversed by paths

in a star-shaped pattern, the points ending with fountains and benches. Light, shade, the sounds of water and birds, and the scurry of lizards are the keys to its enjoyment. Continuing south, one arrives upon a low, round mound planted with salvia and graced by the figure of a huntsman. The only engraving of it shows this mound to be the source of the long, low cascade that follows. (The mound originally was higher, without the huntsman.) Charming statues of pairs of dogs are nearby. The garden, in fact, has a number of live dogs today—chained in various areas. The cascade ends in a deep octagonal basin; beyond are six statues set into hedges leading to the large irregularly shaped fishpond—one of Juvarra's original features. This is surrounded by a balustrade topped with statues.

From here one arrives at the foot of the garden. In the past there was an adjacent sunken garden bordered by hedges with geometric parterres. To the left is a grove of trees sheltering Diana's bath, also by Juvarra. A "ruin" shadows the small murky pond where marble statues of Diana and a nymph swim. There is a legend that these baths are haunted by the white-garbed ghost of Lucida Mansi, who, like Faust, sold her soul to the Devil to preserve her youth and beauty. With the first small wrinkles, the Devil appeared and declared his love, promising her thirty years reprieve from aging in exchange for her soul. She was said to bathe daily here and was known for her nymphomanic tendencies, disposing of her no longer desired lovers by means of a trap door. When the thirty years had passed she retreated alone to her mirrored chamber where her corpse was found riddled with worms. (Albeit dramatic, the tale has no foundation—Lucida Mansi died of the plague with last rites in 1658. The Mansi family did not take possession of the villa until 1675.)

The lawn opens up with a view of the villa and the distant hills beyond. The rear of the villa was redone in the nineteenth century. A garden area against the hillside is planted with tropical plants. A Venus with a dolphin stands on a pedestal from which a mask spouts water into the stagnant pond below.

Towards the entrance of the garden is a Palazzina dell'Orologio built in 1727, probably by Juvarra. Its original appearance is recorded in a painting inside the villa. This clocktower is a unique example of Gothic-Revival in the Lucca territory, with a crenellated rooftop to the rear. This was a multipurpose building serving as stable, armory, dispensary, and ball court.

Today the property has passed to descendants via Signora Laura Salom Mansi to Signor Marino Salom. They have transformed the ground floor of the villa into a restaurant and discotheque.

Villa Reale

Marlia
Gardens open to the public;
music festival in August

Marlia has been fortunate to have had very diligent owners over the centuries. The Orsetti family built the villa in 1651 and retained the property for five hundred years, creating the surviving seventeenth-century portions of the garden. By 1778 it was famed in Europe; copies of its designs were ordered by the Austrian prince Wenzel Anton von Kaunitz. In 1866 Napoleon's sister, Elisa Baciocchi, the princess of Lucca and Piombino, set her heart on acquiring the property. Lelio Orsetti very reluctantly relinquished Marlia, but in protest paraded before the palace an oxcart filled with silver plate —the equivalent of the 700,000 francs Elisa had given him in payment. His messenger informed her that she could see the Villa of Marlia "passing beneath her windows."

The Villa Marlia became Elisa's favorite residence. She had Bienaimé and Lazzarini rebuild the villa and the gate houses (1806–1811) and renamed it Villa Reale Marlia after "Marilla," the ancient name of the district. Elisa loved pomp and established an elaborate minicourt on the grounds, featuring her lover, Signor de Cenami as Grand Master of the Horse, and Niccolo Paganini as her music director. It is said that she fainted in ecstasy hearing Paganini's music, which he played discretely behind a hedge, while she reclined on her chaise longue.

She had grandiose plans for Marlia, which were curtailed only by Napoleon's downfall in 1814 and the arrival of soldiers under Lord William Bentinck. A watercolor plan in the villa illustrates her projected garden, which would have expropriated additional adjacent properties as well as the presently incorporated Villa del Vescovo, a sixteenth-century villa belonging to the local archbishopric which Elisa seized, doubling the pre-existent acreage. Elisa transformed much of the garden into the English landscape style under the guidance of the garden architect Morel. No doubt the surviving Baroque garden rooms would have vanished had she been able to continue. As it was, the vast lawn, the Tuscan *manège,* was extended and softened by the removal of stiff hedges and canals, visible in Francesco Venturi's 1775 engraving. Deer and sheep grazed under laurel, oaks, and a wood of magnolias. A large ornamental lake was added at the bottom of the property. Her hydraulic expenses from 1812 to 1814 were formidable— 438,583 francs.

Of all the owners, Elisa seems to have enjoyed the villa the most. The garden became a shifting setting for her courtiers and their entertainments. One can imagine her acting the title role of *Phèdre* in the green theater, trysting in the upper room of Pan's Grotto, boating in the lake. She must

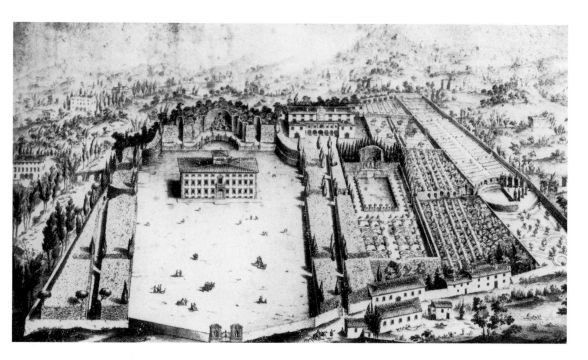

Villa Reale, engraving by
Francesco Venturi (1775).

have recalled the gardens with regret when she was an impoverished refu-
gee in Bologna. In happier days Talleyrand called her "the Semiramis of
the Serchio," after the Serchio River that runs nearby.

After Elisa the villa was given to the Bourbon, Maria Luisa. With the
unification of Italy, the property reverted to the State, and was awarded to
Penelope Smyth, the widow of the prince of Capua. Unfortunately, her son
was institutionalized as insane for thirty years, and the villa was somewhat neglected until 1923, when Count and Countess Pecci-Blunt purchased it. They worked with French landscape architect Gréber to restore
the recent damages, and added a Spanish flower garden and a swimming
pool. The Pecci-Blunt family owns the villa to this day.

Framing the entrance to the villa are two Palladian gatehouses flanking a semicircle which has large Neoclassical urns filled with flowers,
matching those placed on the walkway surrounding the villa.

With the exception of the hillside water theater behind the house, the
garden spreads out on flat terrain. Looking back from the large ornamental
lake, there is a view of the vast expanse of lawn reaching the villa, and the
Pizzorne hills beyond in the distance. It is especially lovely in the autumn
as the park is generously planted with deciduous trees.

On the southeast corner of the property is the small sixteenth-century
bishop's villa (Villa del Vescovo), which was visited by Michel de
Montaigne. It is unusual as it has an inner courtyard, rare in the Lucca
area, and an outer staircase. There is a small formal garden, but its original
garden was lost to Elisa's lawn with the exception of the nearby Grotto
of Pan. This vine-covered pavilion, built between 1570 and 1580, contains
two rooms: one open rectangle on the ground level, with fountain and
seats set into the wall, and a closed chamber in the form of a circular grotto. A loggia room is on the upper floor. A combination of building mate-

rials are used, the floors are patterned pebbles, rough *spugne* covers the walls, and there are motifs of tritons, dophins, and masks. The steps and lower room have outlets for water tricks.

A straight hedge corridor leads to the eighteenth-century Palazzina dell'Orologio, a sizable structure to the east side of the villa. Carrara marble statues are scattered throughout the park, their numbers diminished, many sold, some presently in Derbyshire, England, at Chatsworth.

Marlia's Baroque garden rooms begin with a large enclosed area with a rectangular sheet of water at the north end, set off by a stone balustrade and surmounted by representations of the Arno and Serchio Rivers. Behind them is an elaborately worked stone screen, with an alcove for Leda and her swan, set over a dolphin fountain. The fishpond is a haven for a pair of swans who guard the pots of lemons on the lawn. A flight of steps leads down to a parterred zone. The engraving of 1775 shows an arabesque design. Potted carmine bougainvilleas cut into parasol shapes lead to a pool and fountain in a small niche. John Singer Sargent painted two watercolors (now in the Museum of Fine Arts, Boston) of this garden room.

The real treasure of Marlia is its green theater planted in 1652. Complete in every detail, it has wings and backdrops eighteen feet high, a stage eighty feet deep, a prompter's box, footlights, and orchestra podium—all in topiary; and for the audience—raised grassy tiers, seats marked in Carrara marble slabs, with "boxes" cut in the circular hedges. Terra-cotta actors take their places on the stage, figures from the Italian Commedia dell'Arte: Columbine, Harlequin, Punchinello (before 1925 there were still two other statues of Notaro and Pantaloon).

The approach to the theater is through the gate from the fishpond gardens: a corridor with high hedges, a low flight of stairs, an anteroom with circular low fountain, spurting a tall jet of water in line with the stage seen through the "doors," followed by a second flight of stairs, creating a heightened sense of discovery. Here Jean Racine's *Phèdre* and *Andromache* were performed, as well as Louis Benoît's *La Petite Ville*.

Near the villa are small parterres of ageratum, geranium, and coleus. The villa itself has a severe appearance. It is rectangular, made of buff-colored Tuscan stucco with *pietra serena* (the local gray stone) framed windows, an entrance portico to the rear—not particularly gracious or inviting, nor is it open to the public. To the rear of the villa is one last Baroque element which Elisa didn't change. This is a water theater set into a hill planted with tall ilex. A short water-staircase leads to a terrace on which stand urns and four marble statues. Beneath are masks pouring water into urns, which feed water into an elliptical basin. It is a fitting setting for the Festival of Marlia, that has taken place here in recent years during August focusing on romantic characters such as Figaro, Romeo, Hamlet, and Don Giovanni.

Villa Reale, watercolor by J. C. Shepherd (1925). British Architectural Library, R.I.B.A., London.

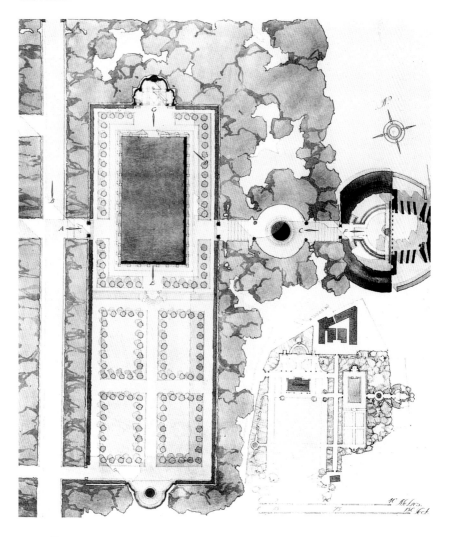

Villa Garzoni

Collodi
Gardens open to the public

The garden of Garzoni at Collodi is the best-known Baroque garden existing today in Tuscany. It sweeps up a hillside like a theater backdrop. Its principal features can be encompassed in one view from the entrance gate. The site and villa-palace have a fairytale quality, heightened by the fact that *L'Avventura di Pinocchio* was conceived by Carlo Lorenzini in the nineteenth century by its kitchen hearth. This fame has been exploited in an overly commercial fashion by the present owners, but fortunately the seventeenth-century lines of the garden, with their eighteenth-century waterworks and statuary, have not been tampered with. It is positioned in a valley between Lucca and Pescia—the Valleriana, a lush fertile zone through which the river Pescia flows.

Originally it was the site of a border castle belonging to Lucca. A condottiere in the employ of Verona and Milan, Count Giovanni Garzoni, citizen of Pescia, first obtained lands in Collodi in 1366 from the monks of Santa Maria Novella and Santa Croce in Valdarno. The former fortress, now in ruins, somehow passed to the Garzoni family, which had by this time severed ties with its native Pescia, rival of Lucca. The original villa of the Garzoni has vanished. The present villa-palace was built by Romano di Alessandro Garzoni, possibly to his own designs, sometime before 1622 when the first honored guests, Ferdinand of Austria, Anna de'Medici, and their daughter visited.

The garden plan developed over twenty years. A drawing depicting the villa in 1633 shows only a bridge spanning the stream; at this time the future garden beyond is only wilderness. A fairly complete description was written in 1692 for an agricultural inventory by Duccino Duccini. Alessandro Garzoni approached Filippo Juvarra for plans in the early eighteenth century; his drawings for unexecuted fountains still exist. Francesco Sbarra's poem, *Le Pompe di Collodi* (1792), described the garden's terraces, plants, and semicircular lower entrance. Romano Garzoni gave the villa its final form at the end of the eighteenth century, working with the architect and man of letters Ottaviano Diodati from Lucca. He designed the charming summer residence behind the palace, planned the waterworks, added the statuary, transformed the parterres from mosaic patterns to the French manner, added the two lower pools, and cut new allées. A detailed design of the garden layout after Diodati's work was made in 1797 by Giuseppe Duggini (now in the Lucca State Archives). The garden was famous beyond the Alps, in part for its visit from the archdukes of Austria. A detailed description written by Francesco Franceschi reached the prince of Kaunitz.

Romano, the proud owner, commissioned an exact engraving of the garden's features for King Stanislas Poniatowski in Warsaw. In Naples King Carlo III summoned Diodati to create the gardens for Caserta based on his success at Collodi (but his project was judged too extravagant and the job in the end went to Luigi Vanvitelli).

Paolo Ludovico Garzoni supposedly played host at Collodi to Napoleon. Through Paolo Ludovico's first wife, Carlotta Venturi of Florence, the villa passed to Senator Giuseppe Garzoni-Venturi, and hence to his daughters, Maria, Marquise Poschi-Meuron, and Emilia San Parravicino who died in 1950 ending the Garzoni line. The villa and garden were then purchased by Count Giancarlo Gardi dell'Ardenghesca of an old Sienese family. He began the restoration and rerouted access to the town, which had previously passed through the grounds of the villa. Now his heirs, Count Guglielmo and Countess Adriana Grazini Gardi have opened the property to the public for tourism, concerts, and conferences.

One enters through the main gate at the bottom of the garden. The villa-palace is not part of the garden composition, but rather is sited off to the left and angled at a higher level. The theater, baths, and promenades were planned to be accessible at the upper levels to accommodate the position of the villa, whereas the lower area was bordered by service buildings, hothouses, and stables. A splendid Baroque set-piece rises up the hillside to dissolve into the surrounding woods. At the lowest level are graceful arabesque parterres, round pools with thirty-foot-high water jets, swans, and lily pads. Gentle ramps run between formal heraldic parterres, with the Garzoni family crest in the center. Following the curves of the walls are

hollowed-out yew hedges, providing a sheltered access to the first terrace level. At ground level there are cages with exotic birds and facilities for refreshments.

Throughout the garden are terra-cotta statues, mostly dating from the eighteenth century—free adaptations of earlier works. The peasant statues are of cruder quality and perhaps date back to the seventeenth century. Most of these statues are mythological figures linked to nature, underlining its transformation and exaltation—Daphne and Apollo, copied loosely after Bernini, showing Daphne's metamorphosis into a laurel bush. Other figures are of Pomona—goddess of tree fruits and gardens; Ceres—goddess of corn; Diana—goddess of woodland and the hunt; Bacchus—god of wine and fertility; fauns; the peasants who work with nature; and personifications of the two rivers that make this valley so fertile.

Arriving below the first terrace, a center niche holds a statue-fountain of a peasant pouring from a barrel. A stately allée of palms marks this level. Figures of *termini* (patron gods of property boundaries) are situated at the ends of the allée. In the center is an octagonal grotto of *spugne*—artificial stalactites—with a statue of Neptune, to whom earthquakes were attributed, riding his seahorse-chariot in the middle niche. This is flanked by niches containing tritons and smaller areas for gargoyle masks. Mosaics cover the floor and archways. Trick waterworks here create surprise jets to bathe the unwary, and a curtain of water closes off the entrance. This grotto was restored in the nineteenth century by the marquis Giuseppe Garzoni. Two small chambers are reached under the stairs; their original use was for food preparation. On top of the terra-cotta balustrades, a group of monkeys plays a ball game. The second level is marked by a se-

ries of busts of nine emperors and eight women, tucked into the hedge. At the far right is a seated statue of Pomona. At the opposite end is a charming green theater, smaller than the one at Marlia, with two marble statues depicting Thalia and Melpomene—the muses of Comedy and Tragedy, plus two elaborate pedestal candelabra composed of dragons spitting flames. A tufa grotto forms the backdrop. Pretty marble benches face the stage where concerts are still given today.

Returning to the center of the second terrace, one should climb the curving staircase adorned with more monkeys. In the center of the double staircase, a cheerful peasant struggles with a spluttering turkey. The side niches contain statues of attendant dogs. At the top, or third level, are two piers with large reclining fauns in tufa. These are genii of the woods, helpers of the shepherds, they are fond of shady, watery, secluded locations. A water cascade continues up the steep hill; moss, ferns, and maidenhair cover the steps. Four large figures of cranes and pelicans play at the bottom. This slope culminates at a large running figure of Fame, the messenger of Jupiter, who holds a trumpet in one hand, and blows a jet of water through a conch shell held in the other. This terra-cotta statue, now badly

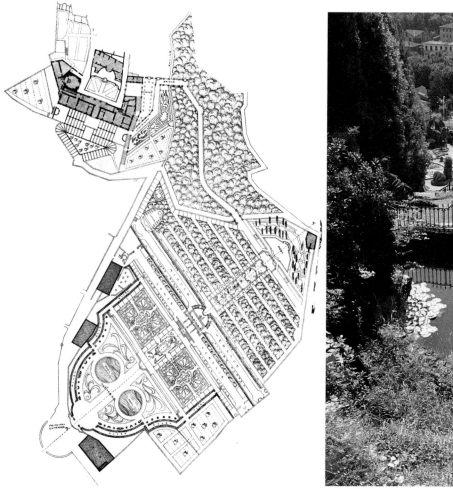

Villa Garzoni, from Triggs, *Art of Garden Design* . . . (1906).

worn, is attributed to Palladini, a sculptor from Lucca. It was added by Diodati, cutting off the former perspective vista. At Fame's feet, a sizable reservoir collects the waters falling from above. Graceless reclining statues, depicting the two rivers—Pescia (with the Florentine Marzocco, or lion) and Collodi (of Lucca)—anchor the composition. Though impressive figures, the statues are more pleasing from afar. Bearing to the right, you come upon a battered figure of a sitting Turk, holding a poppy—the last trace of a former coffee house. If instead you continue west to the left, and then right, you will come to the north end of the garden and the eighteenth-century bath houses. In the seventeenth century there was a hermitage here that Romano Garzoni left undisturbed, its hermit free to wander about the gardens. The present structure was designed by Diodati for socializing while bathing—with screens separating the sexes, a hidden balcony for musicians, and small chambers for dressing and serving snacks. It is perfectly preserved.

Returning the way you came, and bearing right you enter the lane of the camellias—these red and white flowers bloom between February and April. This shady walk leads towards the villa. A stream is spanned by a bridge decorated with mosaics, and statue groupings at either end depict Samson battling the Philistines, and Hercules struggling with the Hydra. The bridge is riddled with water tricks. From it you can look down over the rustic, trapezoidal labyrinth below, which has its own grotto with a peasant emptying a barrel. An angled path follows the side of the labyrinth, and is bordered by five unusual statues of beggars and peasants, giving it the name Viale dei Poveri. This path ends at the entrance of the villa-palace. Here is a large garrison with trophies and enormous statues of amazons and warriors. (The villa itself can be visited, but its secret hanging garden facing northeast is not open to the public.) Descending two flights of steps, which flank the entrance ramps to the villa, one follows a path through a large bamboo grove. A cool spot in the hot summer, the canes here grow up to twelve feet in diameter. The play of light and shade upon the wild violets and cyclamens is particularly agreeable. This grove is traversed by a suspended bridge to a copy of the ancient Uffizi Greek boar, which graces a small fountain. The path leads to the green theater.

Here at Collodi the formal axis of the garden with its Renaissance staircase, is gradually transformed into nature. The clipped hedges meld into the natural woods; the formal balustrades, mosaic-patterned walls, and parterres give way to the rough rockwork of the water-staircase and overall grotto effect at the summit. This transition from formal to wilderness gives the garden its Baroque flavor.

The garden is open daily, year around. The perennials and crocuses start to bloom soon after Christmas, just as the potted orange and lemon trees are brought out. Before March the violets, irises, hyacinths, and primroses flower. And in summer jasmine and musk roses are out. Throughout the garden are palm, oak, and pine trees; box hedges are cut to accomodate the busts; yew hedges define the perimeter of the lower garden; a massive planting of large ilex flanks the water-staircase; and cypresses crown the top of the hill, backing the figure of Fame. Perhaps the loveliest time is in the autumn; the Virginia creeper flames, and the light is particularly enchanting.

Pratolino

Pratolino
Gardens open to the public
on summer weekends

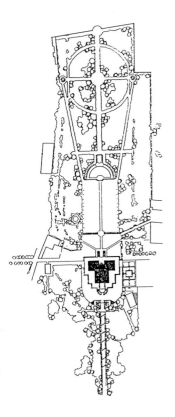

Pratolino, from Shepherd and Jellicoe, *Italian Gardens of the Renaissance* (1925). Courtesy of Academy Editions, London

High above Florence on the Via Bolognese are the rolling fields of Pratolino, formerly a Medici grand ducal villa famed throughout Europe for its fabulous gardens.

The property was bought by Grand Duke Francesco I in 1569 from the estate of Benedetto di Buonaccorso Uguccione. The locals were conscripted to construct the gardens, causing much hardship amongst them. Hauling materials from great distances and excavating a lake in the upper portion of the property strained the men and their beasts. Much previously arable land was now set aside for the park and left uncultivated. Francesco I was a complex character, very unlike his father Cosimo I, the coldly efficient soldier. In 1576, while married to Giovanna of Austria, Francesco met Bianca Cappello, the beautiful runaway wife of a Venetian. Supposedly during this time he fathered a child by her, but there were reports that the labor was false, and Antonio a changeling. They married in 1579. Francesco loved his solitude and used his time away from court duties to pursue his more pressing interests in science and alchemy.

Pratolino was to be used only in the hot summer months. It was conceived of as an evasion from responsibility, reality, and court protocol. The grottoes were designed to cater to Francesco's sense of the fantastic and to provide privacy. Privacy was stressed at Pratolino: a reduced court accompanied the grand duke, and was lodged separately on the grounds. No one entered the guarded property without invitation. Only on the local feast day was the public allowed to enter and admire the gardens and the villa. Special visitors were permitted to come only when the grand duke was not in residence.

Pratolino remained Bianca Cappello's favorite residence. She attracted musicians and poets here, including Torquato Tasso, who wrote this madrigal in 1586 (trans. R. C. Trevelyan, 1871):

> Pleasant and stately grove,
> Your scented foliage spread forth cool and green,
> For here beneath your screen
> This noble maid to couch on grass doth love.
> Together join your boughs, beeches, and firs,
> Ye too link yours together, pine and oak,
> Thou, sacred laurel, and thou myrtle bright:
> Guard from all harm those fairest locks of hers
> And keep her from fierce noonday's fiery stroke;
> Mingle your green with golden glancing light.

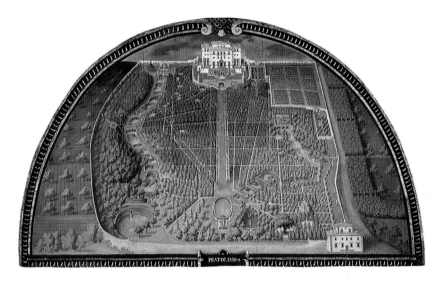

Pratolino, lunette by Giusto Utens (1599), Museo Topografico, Florence.

According to legend, Bianca Cappello enticed her estranged husband to the park for a rendezvous, then set her pet leopard loose in the garden after dark to attack him. (In fact, the inconvenient husband was disposed of in a more conventional manner—knifed by an insulted relative of his mistress.)

Bernardo Buontalenti's design covered the sloping site, with an incline of sixty feet, which leveled out in the center where the villa and its open field was planned. The villa stood between two fir forests, and was designed on an axis that began with the Fountain of Jupiter at the top, passed through the Fountain of the Appennino and its facing *prato* (or field) to the villa, and then continued beyond with an allée cut through a fir forest bordered by a series of gently cascading fountains, to end at the large basin of the Lavandaia (or washwoman).

We have a lunette by Giusto Utens, various prints, and contemporary descriptions to aid us in reconstructing the garden and villa, which were destroyed in the 1820s. Utens' lunette is confusing because of the arbitrary placement of some of the garden features and its omission of the upper portion of the garden, but it is valuable nonetheless for reconstructing the appearance of lost fountains. Of the original garden, only the colossus of Giambologna and a chapel by Buontalenti survive in good condition.

Famed for its water-powered mechanical grottoes, much of Pratolino's fascination remains only in the descriptions of these by visitors and sketches by Buontalenti. The major grottoes were located under the terraces adjoining the villa and were destroyed with the dismantling of the villa in the nineteenth century. Only the Grotto of Cupid and that within the Appennino survive to some degree. The Grotto of Cupid stood to the right of the Lavandaia basin. The exterior had figures of animals and humans worked into its surface. Within a recessed niche a statue of Cupid turned and aimed jets of water, instead of fiery arrows, at the unwary visitor.

The grottoes were numerous, including one of a bear nursing her young. Another, the Fountain of the Flood, had trick thunder, lightning, and rainbows; later this was called the Grotto of the Tritons. One grotto had automations of a knife sharpener, a blacksmith's forge, and an oil press. Yet another grotto by Buontalenti had a piping figure of Pan and a nymph appearing out of the reeds; Galatea rode by on a seashell chariot. At the entrance to the grottoes was an automated swan, which dipped its head into the water.

Francesco's penchant for privacy inspired Buontalenti's Grotto of the Samaritan. Here he could dine with intimates undisturbed by servants. A stone statue of a serving man with a towel draped over his shoulder was mechanized to pour water for the guests from an ewer into a basin. A table of jasper was built over a fountain. At each of the eight settings a disc could be removed to reveal clear cool water below for rinsing fruit, cups, or fingers. In the center was a fountain jet suitable for cooling a bottle. A wheel adjacent to the villa's kitchens facilitated the arrival of food. The hydraulic-powered statue of a woman was added later; at the signal of birds singing and a bagpipe playing, she advanced, dipped her bucket into a well, then retreated to a loggia. Above her moved a hunting scene.

Such a wealth of fantasy, or *meraviglie,* was in keeping with the theatrical spirit of the times. Buontalenti, it must be remembered, was not only an architect, but also a set designer. Because he was practically illiterate, it is most probable that the themes for the park were suggested by the grand duke himself. If there is a central program it must be of the energy of water, and the ambiguity of the real and the unreal.

Giambologna's fabulous giant, the Appennino—referring to the mountain range on which Pratolino sits—remains intact on its original site. A huddled ambiguous figure, its texture suggests the Appennine mountains: rough, hoary, craggy, crouching, pressing down into the earth. Water flowed down the shaggy beard into the lily pond.

The interior is hollow; three men could stand within the head and look through the open eyes. A grotto with skylight is in the central portion. It contains a statue of Venus and an enormous branch of coral from the Red Sea, which once served as a fountain. At a later date, Giovan Battista Foggini added a winged dragon behind the head, which spewed water from its mouth. This statue has become a symbol of the garden.

A large statue of Perseus dominating a spouting dragon stood near the Appennino. The octagonal chapel by Buontalenti in this area remains intact, set up on a platform, nestled in the woods with a tiny graveyard of the Demidoff family behind it. Also to the west of the villa was the Fountain of the Mask, whose waters descended through a series of fishponds. At the bottom was the Fountain of the Calciuoli, edged with bronze satyrs by Giambologna—it is now in the Palazzo del Bargello.

To the east, level with the villa's terrace, was a large sunken aviary; only the foundations are visible today. In this area there was a secret garden with a columned fountain. Set in a clearing was the Fountain of the Rovere; an ancient oak (or *rovere*) had a staircase entwined around it, leading to a platform with a table and fountain. Beyond it stood the artificial Mount of Parnassus, studded with marble statues of muses, at the top Apollo played his harp with winged Pegasus. (Pegasus and one of the seated muses are now in Boboli.) Inside the mount was a hydraulic organ.

The central viale from the terraces through the fir forest to the basin of the Lavandaia, was edged by a series of fountains. The over-life-size statue of the Lavandaia wrung out a tablecloth with water streaming from it into the large basin below. Next to her stood a small child urinating. Near them was a basin with bubbling water.

It is unknown how many statues were in the garden, but certainly many were stolen or destroyed. Fortunately some of the best were transported to Boboli, including that of the Aesculapius, god of healing.

The Grotto of the Mugnone which stood between the stairway leading to the villa terraces was restored inaccurately by Maria Demidoff. Its statue of the river Mugnone was pieced together. The Fountain of the Mask was also reconstructed, but the Mask, or "Pan," is a modern work.

On the large terrace of the villa were installed the statues of the important fountain Bartolommeo Ammannati built for the Salone dei Cinquecento of Palazzo Vecchio. Here the figures stood without the huge linking marble arch until 1590, when they were again moved, this time to Boboli. At present they are in the courtyard of the Palazzo del Bargello.

A separate lodge, the Paggeria, housed the pages and courtiers. This eventually became the nucleus of the Villa Demidoff. There was also the Quartiere del Fontaniere, a special building to contain the many valves of the intricate waterworks.

Bianca Cappello's son, Antonio, was passed over for both the succession to the throne and the possession of Pratolino. Instead, Francesco's brother, Cardinal Ferdinando de'Medici was made grand duke. Later, under Prince Ferdinando's tenure, Pratolino acquired a theater within the villa. Giuseppe Scarlatti created five operas for its stage. Pratolino's decline can be marked with the advent of the Lorraine dynasty when the last of the Medici, Gian Gastone, died in 1737. The throne passed to Francesco Stefano, duke of Lorraine. Shortly thereafter he became emperor and never visited Florence, except once in 1739. At that time he came to Pratolino, and it is probable that the hydraulic grottoes functioned for the last time for his visit. The villa was neglected, and the property was rented to Bernardo Sgrilli for nine years. He described Pratolino fully in *Descrizione della Regia Villa, Fontane e Fabbriche di Pratolino*, published in Florence in 1742. The next grand duke, Pietro Leopoldo, turned to public works and considered the maintenance of Pratolino an extravagance. During the tenure of the first Lorraine grand dukes, the neglected waterworks deteriorated, and water seeped through the pipes undermining the foundations of the villa. This was the ultimate cause of the destruction of Buontalenti's villa. The young grand duke Ferdinando III had intentions of restoring the villa. At the urging of a Bohemian engineer, Joseph Fichs, work began in 1821 to dismantle the villa. Fichs redesigned the park, creating a new network of curving paths in the English style, and planted specimen trees, including many horse chestnuts. After the untimely death of Ferdinando in 1824 the project was abandoned. In 1872 it was sold to Prince Paul Demidoff di San Donato.

Demidoff enlarged the existing Paggeria as a residence. His widow gave the villa to their daughter Maria in 1903, who herself was widowed in 1916 when her husband was killed by the Bolsheviks in Russia. Maria remained a recluse within the walls of Pratolino, restoring the grounds. The city of Florence purchased the estate several years ago.

The park remains hauntingly beautiful, vast and sprawling, with magnificent old trees, open meadows, and cool woodland paths.

Villa di Castello

At first glance, the Medici villa of Castello strikes the viewer as barren, a large graceless edifice. It is occupied today as an elementary school, various apartments, and storerooms. For the visitor, the garden seems to hold out little promise. However, beyond the transformed side areas and somewhat altered central garden is an exceptionally beautiful Renaissance fountain and two stupendous works of whimsy: a grotto full of animals and a giant huddled on an island. Castello is open to the public, yet has fewer visitors than it merits. One can wander peacefully within its walled garden, jarred only by the piercing closing-hour whistle of the caretaker.

In its day, this was one of the foremost gardens of Europe, a trendsetter visited by Michel de Montaigne in 1580 and 1581, and by the French botanist-zoologist Pierre Belon, who listed its exotic plants when he saw it between 1546 and 1549. Yet many of the garden details were never completed. It is believed that the original conception is that of the historian Benedetto Varchi, who worked out a complex iconographical scheme to be executed by the architect-sculptor Niccolò Tribolo. Unfortunately, the artist died in 1550, leaving the work half completed. Bernardo Buontalenti took over as director of the work force, very probably imposing his own ideas and modifying the first conception. He was assisted by Bartolommeo Ammannati, Perino del Vaga, Valerio Cioli, Giambologna, and Stoldo and Antonio Lorenzi—the finest sculptors in Florence at the time.

Lorenzo and Giuliano di Pierfrancesco de'Medici acquired the villa in 1477. They belonged to the cadet branch of the powerful Medici family. When Pietro de'Medici was driven out of Florence in 1494 for allowing King Charles VIII of France to pass through the city, Lorenzo and Giuliano allied themselves to the popular party; this action preserved much of the villa's contents while other Medici properties were looted. Lorenzo was a primary patron of Botticelli's; the painter created for him the *Birth of Venus, Primavera, Pallas and the Centaur,* as well as the illustrations to Dante's *Divina Commedia.* The large canvases remained safely in the villa until 1815, when they were transferred to the Galleria degli Uffizi.

Grand Duke Cosimo I chose Castello as his retirement home. After successfully reshaping the Florentine state from chaos, he put in order the villa's garden and cultivated jasmine. The garden's creation dates from Cosimo's time. It is he who commissioned Tribolo in 1537 to rebuild the villa, and following that to create the garden.

When you visit Castello a main road passes directly in front of the villa. This is typical of Italian villa design, which set aside the maximal area for the private use of the garden behind the villa. There is an oval piazza in front of the villa, and a row of trees stretching south towards the river. Originally the villa was known as "Il Vivaio," for the enormous rectangular fishpond that extended the villa's length. This pond was bridged in the center, and was on an axis with the allée. Tribolo planned this to be of pleached mulberry trees, forming a tunnel extraordinary in length—over a mile—to the banks of the Arno. This was to have been flanked by narrow side canals, and would have been the first Renaissance garden with waterways. The perspective allée leading to the river, and the placement of the villa above a fishpond, were features also present in the earlier gardens of the Quaracchi, located nearby. The site begins at the foot of Monte Morello, and gently slopes up the hillside, affording views over the valley.

Right:
Villa di Castello, from Triggs, *Art of Garden Design . . .* (1906).

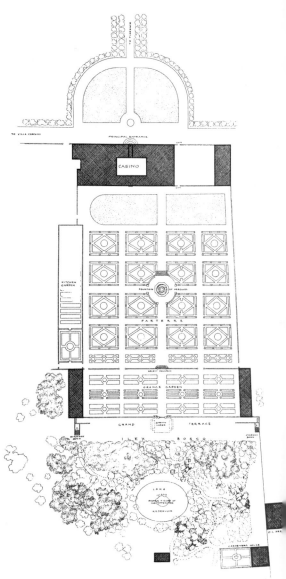

The garden is divided into terraces taking advantage of this natural formation.

Benedetto Varchi's plan set forth the natural forces of the garden's creation: the four seasons, the rivers—source of water supplying the fountains, and symbolic of the fertility of the Florentine valley—and the mountains surrounding the site, while at the same time glorifying his Medici patrons by alluding to their territorial possessions. In further tribute to the family under whose rule Florence became a leading center of the arts and sciences, Varchi personified the Virtues as individual members of the family, mirrored on the opposite walls by the disciplines they promoted. The subject matter of the statuary was not haphazard, but followed a set scheme which would have been readable to those of a Renaissance education. This is the first garden of its type in the Renaissance to be so unified in its intent. Allegorical schemes had been depicted in the past within the villa, here for the first time an allegorical program is moved into the garden. Ancient statues were excluded from the garden, unlike the majority of Renaissance gardens. Now, for the first time, contemporary sculptures that were not merely fountain figures were commissioned for a garden. Unfortunately, today most of the statuary of Villa di Castello has been removed to museums or to other Medici gardens.

In the area behind the villa is a walled enclosure of a broad flowered terrace. In 1895 when the American landscape architect Charles Platt saw this he was struck by the profusion of flowers, and the walls of roses, with grapevines strung horizontally above them. In Vasari's time the garden walls were covered with espaliered bitter oranges and pomegranates. Today there are still flowers here, but fewer. In the center where formerly a circular labyrinth of bay and myrtle stood surrounded by cypresses, is now the tall Fountain of Hercules. This fountain group was designed by Tribolo and cast by Ammannati in 1550. The shaft is carved by Tribolo, the four bronze nude boys were modeled by him, and the other portions are by Valerio Cioli, Perino del Vaga, Stoldo and Antonio Lorenzi. This light-hearted confection was surmounted by the struggling bronze figures of Hercules and Antaeus, water gushing from the throat of the choking Antaeus, who is losing strength as he is lifted from the earth, his source of power. These figures were removed recently for restoration.

The four Roman statues facing the fountain were positioned here at a later date. Originally this was the location of the Fountain of Fiorenza. This charming marble and bronze fountain has since been moved to the neighboring Medici villa, La Petraia, and rechristened the Fountain of Venus. These two fountains—of Fiorenza and Hercules—surpassed in richness of design all previous fountains.

In the center of the north wall is a deeply recessed grotto, bordered by Tuscan columns. Within is an enchanted world. The floor is tesselated, concealing trick water jets. Colored shell patterns of arabesques and masks decorate the ceiling. The three tufa walls each have a fantastic assemblage of life-size animals surmounting the marble basins, which teem with sea creatures, coral branches, and shells. Upon hearing of the grand duke's intent to build fountains, the architect Antonio da Sangallo wrote to him in 1546 from Rome, mentioning that Roman gardens often featured grottoes, inspired by the discovery of those at the Villa of Volpischios, which were decorated with stalactitelike stones. Here the grotto has fake stalactites in tufa, and fostered a fashion in Tuscan gardens in imitation of the Roman style. The animals were made after Tribolo's death, and are possibly by the sculptor Giovanni di Paolo Fancelli. When Vasari described the grotto in 1568, he mentioned only the carved marine basins; therefore the animals probably date from between 1568 and 1580. The animals are of colored marbles and stone with traces of paint. The stag has real horns and the wild boar, real tusks. Badger, cat, weasel, gazelle, ram, ox, rabbit, lion, panther, rhinoceros, and unicorn—all make up a Renaissance bestiary. In addition, superb realistic bronze birds by Giambologna were perched on the rockery walls. (These are now in the Palazzo del Bargello.)As travel increased, exotic animals found their places in the zoos of the Italian courts. But, because everything was deliberate in the planning of the garden, we must look for an explanation of this display. Liliane Chatelet-Lange has produced the most logical ("Grotto of the Unicorn and the Garden of the Villa di Castello," *Art Bulletin*, March, 1908). She recounts the legend of how all the beasts came to drink at the lake, when a snake appeared and contaminated the waters with its poison. The animals waited until the unicorn came and, by dipping his horn in the waters, made them pure again. Here the white marble unicorn stands out as the central figure, and the inference is clear—that the waters of Castello are pure.

Water was first supplied to the villa by a Roman aqueduct. Tribolo, with the assistance of Piero da San Casciano, had the task of increasing the waters for the elaborate waterworks projected. Water was diverted from Castellina and La Petraia to be collected in a reservoir on the topmost terrace. The water passed through the grotto to the Fountains of the Arno and Mugnone, then dripped down the river gods' beards to the Fountain of Fiorenza, and further down to the Fountain of Hercules and Antaeus, filling the fishponds. Whatever remained was used to fill the canals running into the Arno River.

Climbing to the top terrace by either of the staircases flanking the grotto, one enters a dark grove of ilex, fir, cypress, and laurel—a shady contrast to the sun-drenched, walled garden below. This wilderness is largely untouched. Set in the center of the reservoir on a rocky moss-covered mass is a large bronze crouching figure of an old man, representing the Appennine mountains. Small jets of water issue out of the crown of his head and droplets ooze down his body to suggest tears and sweat, but the effect is more that of a man enduring a chilling shower. This statue was made by Ammannati, probably after Tribolo's sketch.

Originally the villa was flanked by small walled enclosures, secret gardens for growing herbs. A large orchard extended to the western border of the property, while to the east were other smaller formal gardens, including a pavilion and plantations of apples and firs. It appears that there were two further reservoirs in the side sections.

Under Cardinal Gian Carlo de'Medici, Villa di Castello hosted many festivities. The pleasure-loving cardinal eventually ran through his patrimony and died here. Because Castello was a favorite Medici villa, it was kept up until the Savoys ruled Florence. In the late eighteenth century Grand Duke Pietro Leopoldo radically transformed the gardens, destroying the eastern portions to replant in the English style, covering up the *vivaio* in front, and removing the maze and the small walled herb gardens.

In its day, Castello was an inspiration for gardens throughout Europe for its iconography, layout, and the outstanding quality of its sculpture.

Villa della Petraia

Castello
Gardens open mornings
to the public
(closed Mondays)

Practically adjacent to the Villa di Castello is Villa della Petraia, also a Medici property. While Castello lies at the foot of the hillside, its facade right up against the main road and its gardens concealed behind the villa in typical Tuscan fashion, La Petraia sits upon the upper heights of the hillside, surveying the view of the Arno valley far below, the gardens spread conspicuously beneath the villa's upper terrace.

The core of the villa was a fourteenth-century fortress, of which only the tower remains; it has a family resemblance to the tower of Palazzo Vecchio at Florence. In 1427 the villa was confiscated from its rebel owner, Palla di Noteri Strozzi. It was acquired by Benedetto d'Antonio Salutati for 23,070 scudi from the Florentine government. The Medici were the subsequent owners. Cardinal Ferdinando de'Medici hired Bernardo Buontalenti to enlarge and improve the property around 1575. It became the favorite retreat of Grand Duke Cosimo I, the cardinal's father. At this time La Petraia was used basically as a hunting lodge. The Italian State took over the property in 1859 under King Vittorio Emanuele II. The king was particularly fond of the villa, but unfortunately modified it and its gardens. During Florence's brief period as capital of Italy, he spent as much time as possible here with his morganatic wife, "La Bella Rosina," countess of Mirafiori. Later when he moved to the Quirinale, he had flowers cut daily at La Petraia and sent to Rome.

One enters by a side road scaling the hillside, lined with gardeners' cottages. Through the garden wall is a shady *bosco* of ilex, and low, box-bordered flower beds across the sloping, wide rectangular lower area. In the center, on a slight mound reached by steps, is a simple three-tiered fountain surrounded by a circular hedge. This fountain and a double flight of steps rising to the next level are on an axis with the buff-colored, two-storied square villa, its defense tower jutting above the roof line.

The second terrace has a long, broad fish tank filled with enormous carp. Pink geraniums line the staircase, which crosses over the tank and leads to the top level, where the villa is set between lawns. On this terrace, a ninteenth-century corner loggia faces southeast towards Florence. The gem of this setting is Tribolo's marble fountain, originally at the Villa di Castello, moved here by Grand Duke Pietro Leopoldo. Of this fountain Giorgio Vasari wrote (*Le Vite de'più eccelenti architetti, pittori ed scultori italiani*, trans. A. B. Hinds, 1963):

> He next began the fountain of the labyrinth, making marine monsters encircling the base, in marble, so carved with their tails intertwined that it is a

unique work of its kind. He then did the marble basin, first carried out at Castello, with a large marble bas-relief. . . . Before making the basin Tribolo did some cherubs dancing to decorate this, holding festoons of marine objects beautifully carved. He also gracefully executed the cherubs and masks for spouting water, and proposed to erect a bronze statue three braccia high on the top, to represent Florence, to which the waters of the Arno and Mugnone flow. For this figure he had made a fine model, which was to wring water out of its hair.

Attributed to Giambologna, the graceful figure of Florence wringing her hair was removed in the 1980s for a restoration show, and has yet to be reinstalled.

Set in a *bosco* to the left of the villa is a huge ilex containing a platform tree house, where Vittorio Emanuele and Rosina often dined *al fresco*. Behind the villa is a dark curtain of cypresses; a few are ancient and are believed to have been planted by the Romans when they built a road here to link Florence with Bologna.

You are apt to encounter wedding couples being photographed, but few other visitors come to disturb the quiet of this garden.

Villa Corsi-Salviati

Sesto
Gardens open upon request:
Conti Corsi-Salviati
Via Gramsci
Sesto (Florence)

or with Agritourist tours:
Via Proconsolo, 10
Florence

Villa Corsi-Salviati is an example of a garden created and continually altered by generations of the same family. The gardens have been the glory of the villa since the late sixteenth century. Set on flat terrain at Sesto, a suburb of Florence, Villa Corsi-Salviati does not have the descending terraces or sweeping views enjoyed by other Tuscan villas. What it still maintains in great part is a series of linked garden-rooms within a large walled rectangle behind the villa.

An old farm house was bought by Simone Corsi in 1502 from Andrea Carnesecchi; of this no trace remains; the structure has been enlarged gradually since 1532 beyond recognition. A small fresco inside the villa painted by Bernardino Poccetti in the sixteenth century shows a very simple garden of square beds with a fountain. At the end of the sixteenth cen-

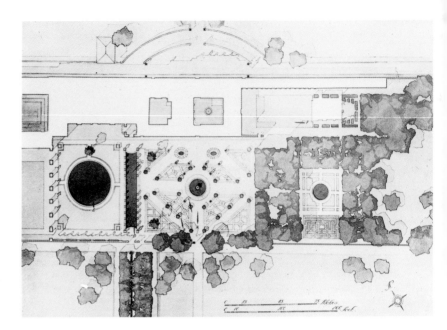

Villa Corsi-Salviati, watercolor by J. C. Shepherd (1925). British Architectural Library, R.I.B.A., London.

tury the garden was divided into well-defined sections, the first composed of formal symmetrical square beds around a central fountain with two smaller fountains flanking the main door of the villa. (This area remains a strictly formal garden today.) The second zone is to the west of the central garden, consisting of a fishpond set off by looming stuccoed portals and balustrade. The fishpond originally had a convex west wall, with a grotto and statue. Beyond was a third section featuring a *leporarium*, or moated rabbit island, against the garden wall. This area also served as a lemon garden. To the east of the central parterre was a walled-in *bosco*, leading to an *orto*, or orchard, enclosed on three sides; at the fourth was a lemon *stanzone*. Behind the *bosco* and *orto* was a bowling green flanking a long narrow wing of the villa. The entire eastern portion of the garden is now greatly changed. An extensive *ragnaia*, or hunting wood, still stretches between the garden gate and the river.

The marquis Antonio di Giovanni Corsi initiated plans to bring additional water to the garden in 1676. The villa in the late seventeenth century was a long, two-storied structure, built around a central courtyard with four square crenellated corner towers. In 1738 the marquis Antonio transformed the facade into the Baroque style. He also removed the dividing garden walls, changed the rabbit island in 1708 into a circular lake with water jets, and altered the fishpond into a long rectangular canal, decorated with urns and statues of the four seasons. In the parterre garden, the box square beds took on their diamond-shapes as seen now. The large birdcages attached to the villa were converted into open, frescoed loggias. All this remains today. In addition, he expanded the *bosco* into the former orchard, planting it with ilex; some of the trees still survive. The *ragnaia* was destroyed, replaced by a long narrow cascade-canal bordered by shady viales of ilex and laurel. The cascade began with a basin decorated with dolphins and continued for nearly one thousand feet flowing through thirteen sections with jets, ending in a *trompe l'oeil* design decorated with *spugne* and mosaic that suggested even further depth. The only part of the garden the marquis Antonio left untouched was the bowling green. Giuseppe Zocchi's print made between 1733 and 1750 shows the finished product of the marquis's labors (he died in 1743).

Gradually in the eighteenth century the garden was decorated with urns, stone balustrades, and wrought-iron gates topped with statuary—wonderful figures of dogs, peasants, and dragons.

The nineteenth century brought the inevitable English landscape transformations, fortunately relegated to the eastern portion of the garden beyond the ilex *bosco*. In 1815 Marquis Amerigo Corsi pulled down the dividing walls separating the orchard from the parterrre and central basin. Two years later he constructed the artificial lake with its island and rustic hut.

He added two mounts, one called "Montagnole" with a little fortress over a rock from which a spring supplied water for the lake. By 1845 the old box design of the parterre and the proportions of its basin were changed. Tall trees including palms were put in this central area. The parterre design was much simplified, box borders swept away, and pebbles put in their place. By the mid-nineteenth century the garden took on importance for its botanical developments. Two new exotic hothouses featured succulents, camellias, and rare examples of carnations, Granducal and Goa jasmine, and a large ranunculus known as Roselline di Firenze. The marquis Bardo Corsi-Salviati's passion for tropical plants dates from 1866; from May to October they were transplanted from the hothouses to the garden beds.

In 1907 the marquis Giulio Corsi-Salviati began to restore the garden to its earlier state, basing the design on a plan of the garden as it appeared at the end of the seventeenth century. He removed two greenhouses and

Villa Corsi-Salviati, engraving by G. Zocchi (18th century).

most of the palm trees, replanted the central parterre in its diamond pattern, and restored the aviary. The eastern section was reordered for clarity. A grotto and mount were removed. The area of the original *orto* was divided with straight paths to a central basin, surrounded by simple geometric parterres. A statue by Antonio Berti of the marquis's young daughter Anna graced the fountain. Among his major innovations were a new labyrinth, a green theater, and a tennis court (well hidden beyond the lake). The labyrinth was based on Hampton Court's in Middlesex, England. It still exists today, in box reaching to about five and one-half feet in height, but so densely overgrown that it is becoming difficult to make out its narrow corridors. The green theater was patterned after that of Mirabelle Castle at Salzburg. It is charming and neatly kept up. Cypresses mark the stage's corners and loom behind it. Box hedges form the backdrop and the wings, four on each side. The prompter's box is also of boxwood, with sunken pit to stand in. A classical statue of Apollo stands on a base at the back of the stage. This formerly stood on the villa's rooftop until toppled by a strong wind. Grassy lawns face the theater. Against the *limonaia* are marble statues of putti, Adonis, Diana, Lucretia, and Cleopatra. Trellised roses and potted lemons add to the charm.

The eastern portion of the garden, with the exception of the green theater, is in a state of neglect. The lake area is strewn with rubble and building materials. The little parterre in the former *orto* is untended; modern tables and chairs are set out there for the students. The statue of Anna Guicciardini has been removed. The head gardener implied that the visiting scholars were expected to remain in the eastern portion of the garden. It is hoped that eventually this area will be spruced up when renovations to the villa are completed. The central portion of the garden fares better— its flower beds are maintained. Roses and wisteria grow against the villa's walls. Orange and lemon trees in pots are still trundled out according to the season. May and September are the best months to view this garden. No hint of it is gleaned from the street; bus drivers draw a blank when asked about the villa's location which is on their route, yet the villa is reawakening to activity, bringing the outer world within its walls. Special photography shows are displayed within the *limonaia*; the Smithsonian Institution uses the villa to host a summer lecture series, and the University of Michigan has a Florentine program housed here. The villa is now owned by the marquis Giulio's sons, the counts Roberto and Giovanni Guicciardini Corsi-Salviati.

Leaving the busy street, in what has become a nondescript suburb, one passes through the tall cool hall of the villa, across a courtyard to an oasis of sunlight, its peace and quiet broken only by the sound of the birds and croaking of frogs among the lily pads. Stretching beyond the parterre gateway is an expanse of undeveloped countryside, and one cannot but marvel at the contrast to the noisy world outside the villa.

Villa Medici

Fiesole
Gardens open upon request:
Signora Anna Mazzini
Villa Medici
Via Vecchia Fiesolana
Fiesole

The old approach road to Fiesole, the Vecchia Fiesolana, rises and twists until it reaches a gate set off by cypresses and a fountain. Driving past, concentrating on the steepness and narrowness of the road, it is easy to overlook the old fifteenth-century villa nestled against the hillside, its garden hidden behind high walls. This is the famous Villa Medici, one of the few Medician villas now held in private ownership and inhabited.

Michelozzo Michelozzi built the villa for Giovanni de'Medici. Giorgio Vasari extolled its design in his life of Michelozzo in *Le Vite de'piu eccelenti architetti, pittori, ed scultori italiani* (trans. A. B. Hinds, 1963):

> For Giovanni, the son of Cosimo de'Medici, he made another magnificent palace at Fiesole, the foundation being dug in the sides of the hill, at a great expense, but not without great advantage, as he utilised the basement for the vaults, larders, stables, butteries and other convenient things. Above, besides the usual chambers, halls and other apartments, he made some for books and others for music; in fine, in this building Michelozzo displayed to the full his ability as an architect. The building, besides what I have said, was so excellently constructed that it has never stirred a hair's-breadth.

The villa still sits solidly on its foundations, but has been considerably altered and expanded. The width of the villa has been enlarged towards the hillside; service rooms such as the kitchen have been moved up from the basements for greater convenience.

Leon Battista Alberti's treatise on architecture was first issued in 1452. In it he recommends building a villa on a site very much like this. This is an early attempt at planning an axial garden on a limited, narrow site: the main terrace aligned with the loggia, and the steps descending from the pergola into the formal garden to the central fountain, lead to the view beyond. The systematic planning of hillside terracing for a garden would become a major feature of Italian gardens, following the example of Villa Medici.

It is difficult to say with precision which portions of this garden are original—Cecil Pinsent and Geoffrey Scott revamped the design in this century—but the various levels undoubtedly existed in the time of Lorenzo il Magnifico (d. 1492). The layout of the splendid cypress walk beyond the terraces, and very probably the existence of a pergola and raised flower bed behind it, also date from the end of the fifteenth century. Tucked below the villa in the secret garden, with its box hedges, simple fountain, and stone seats overlooking the Arno valley, the ties to the Renaissance are strongest.

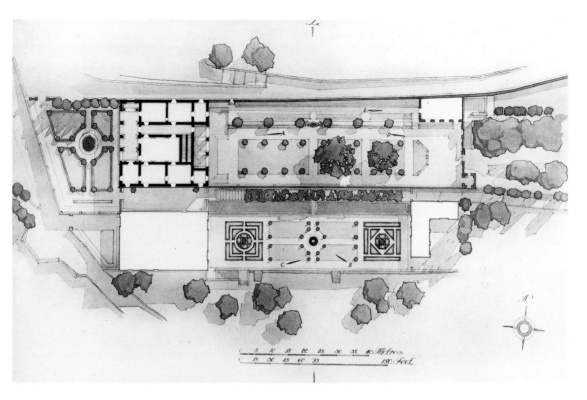

Villa Medici, watercolor
by J. C. Shepherd (1925).
British Architectural Library, R.I.B.A., London.

The loggia opens onto the main terrace, a long rectangle. Down the center is a lawn planted with two ancient shady *Paulownias*—lovely in the spring with their blue blossoms. This lawn was undoubtedly a parterre in the past. Towards the hillside is a long, raised rose bed ending in a lemon house covered with white blossoming vines. It has been suggested that this raised flower garden was added later when the villa was widened in the eighteenth century. Hydrangeas and a large potted azalea add seasonal color. At the far end are two double niches covered with pebble mosaicwork; the one towards the city features a fresco of a lady. Between the niches a path leads through to the spectacular cypress walks, and a staircase, which runs up behind the lemon house leads to a grassy overgrown area, perhaps originally a bowling green.

The cypress allée curves about leading to the lower terrace, otherwise accessible from the villa's basement. Against the retaining wall is a pergola with a row of hydrangeas. The pergola's original posts have been substituted, and white flowered vines cover the trellis. From its center, steps descend to a more formal garden, which is also a rectangular terrace, planted with sectional box parterres filled with flowers. Tubs of geraniums and lemon trees surround the garden; a magnolia tree provides shade. Below this are fields of olive trees. Of the orchards and vegetable gardens of Lorenzo's day there are no traces. Following through the pergola to the west is the secret garden of box hedges and magnolias and a small stone fountain, where black squirrels play. Slightly below it, accessible only through a building that borders the formal garden, a small wedge-shaped garden with an arbor and stone benches is placed to enjoy the view.

The property was first owned by the Baldi family who sold it in 1458 to one of the founders of the Medici dynasty, Cosimo the Elder. The Medici held it for two hundred years, calling it Villa Belcante. Cardinal Raffaello Riario, Pope Sixtus IV's nephew, planned to assassinate his host Giuliano and Lorenzo il Magnifico at a meal here, but pre-warned, they excused themselves from appearing. By the end of the seventeenth century, during the time of Grand Duke Cosimo III, it was considered an insignificant property, too small for entertaining on the scale the Medici were then accustomed to, so it was sold off to Vincenzo di Cosimo del Sera in 1671 for four thousand scudi. (The del Sera coat-of-arms is still over the loggia.) In 1721 it was inherited by the Durazzini, who sold it four years later to the Borgherini. When this family died out in 1771 it was purchased by Albergotto Albergotti, who sold it the following year to Margherita Rolle, widow of the English statesman, Sir Robert Walpole. Subsequently it was owned by the Mozzi, Spence, and MacCalman families. The writer Iris Origo brought it to her marriage as her dowry. It is now the home of Aldo Mazzini's widow, Anna, and their children.

The garden is an intimate one, not planned for large receptions or to impress by splendor or novelty. It has always served as a retreat from the restless city of Florence below it, a place for contemplation and relaxation. In the time of Lorenzo il Magnifico it was the meeting place of the Platonic Academy: Angelo Poliziano, Pico della Mirandola, and Marsilio Ficino gathered here to read and discuss their works and formulate the philosophy of Neoplatonism. Poliziano was appointed tutor to Lorenzo's son in the fall of 1478, but his temperament clashed with Clarice Orsini's, the

boy's mother. During his time at Fiesole he wrote the Latin poem "Rusticus" describing the view from the garden and the winding avenue. The following year the children and Clarice moved to Careggi, and Ficino became their tutor, leaving Poliziano in blessed peace at Villa Medici. That summer Poliziano wrote to his friend Ficino (C. Latham, *The Gardens of Italy*, 1905):

> When Careggi becomes too hot in August I hope you may not think this our rustic dwelling of Fiesole beneath your notice. We have plenty of water here, and as we are in a valley, but little sun, and never without a cooling breeze. The villa itself lying off the road and almost hidden in the midst of a wood, yet commands a view of the whole of Florence and altho in a densely populated district, yet I have perfect solitude such as is loved by him who leaves the town. But I will tempt of thee with yet another attraction. Pico sometimes wanders beyond the limit of his own grounds, breaks in unexpectedly on my solitude and carries me away from my shady garden to his evening meal.

In recent years, Prince Charles has twice visited the gardens, finding them restful after his official duties. The gardens and the loggia (the grotesques on the vaulted ceiling just restored) have a lived-in family feeling. The terraces and shady walks lack the stiffness found in other historic Italian gardens. The gardens are maintained, but not impeccably, compared to those of nearby Gamberaia, owned by Signora Mazzini's father. The views of Florence are superlative and can be enjoyed from every portion of the garden. The hamlet of San Domenico lies below, at just the right distance from the terraces.

Villa Palmieri

Fiesole
Gardens open upon request:
Signora Bellandi
Via Boccaccio, 128
Fiesole

or with Agritourist tours:
Via Proconsolo, 10
Florence

Boccaccio's *Decameron* is set during the raging plague of 1348 in a garden outside of Florence. On the third day of his flight from Florence, Neifile leads seven maidens and their accompanying three gentlemen to a villa believed to be situated on the site of the present-day Villa Palmieri. They "spared not to say; if any paradise remained in earth to be seen, it could not possibly be in any other place, but only was contained within the compass of this garden" (trans. R. Aldington, 1930). It is known through documents in the State Archives that Boccaccio's father owned property in the vicinity of Villa Palmieri.

The fine villa described in the *Decameron* was on a hillside, with a colonnade for dining, a walled garden, and grape-arbored walks leading to "a square plot resembling a meadow, flourishing with high grass, herbs, and plants, besides a hundred diversities of flowers, looking as if they had been planted there," surrounded by cypresses and orange trees. In the center was a white marble pedestal fountain with a standing figure, the water channeled off throughout the garden and descended underground to twin mills. "Keen was their enjoyment as they sauntered about, wreathing their heads with flowers, and listening to the birds sing melodiously." The "Cento Novelle" of the *Decameron* were told at banqueting tables placed around the fountain.

Nothing remains of the medieval garden carefully described by Boccaccio, except perhaps the two mills, the sloping hillside, and the view across the Arno valley encompassing the Bargello and Badia towers within the city.

Accuracy apart, it is an evocative description of a princely villa of the era. If indeed it was Villa Palmieri, the property and the villa built in 1259 belonged at the end of the plague to Cioni de Fini. By 1350 it was purchased by the noble Nuccio Solosmei, and took the name of Villa Tre Visi. This villa has vanished. His descendant Matteo Solosmei sold it in 1454 to the rich pharmacist Marco Palmieri. Palmieri's son, Matteo, famed intellectual, was a member of the Neoplatonist circle of Cosimo de'Medici the Elder; among his writings was the Dantesque poem, "Città di Vita," for which he was declared a heretic after his death. It spoke of pre-existence of the soul, which was unacceptable to the church. The poem, written between 1541 and 1565, narrowly escaped destruction, and is found today, in the Laurentian Library. A patron of the arts, he commissioned an Assumption of the Virgin with portraits of himself and his wife, Cosa Serragli, by Raffaelo di Francesco Botticini (not Botticelli as Vasari stated). This was in the family chapel of San Pietro Maggiore until the controversy broke over his poem, and the donor figure was slashed. The painting was then removed to Villa Palmieri and walled up. (It is now in the National Gallery of Art, London.) In 1697 Palmiero Palmieri altered the house and grounds substantially, basically giving the house its present appearance. Palmiero created the loggia, enclosing the impressive three-sided courtyard.

The only remaining traces of the old garden date from this period. This is the enclosed oval lemon garden to the south of the house. The broad balustraded terrace in front of the villa is connected by sweeping ramp-stairs leading down to the lemon garden. These stairs extended over the old road to Fiesole, which bisected the property as seen in Zocchi's print of the villa. The brick-patterned terraces are studded with statues and

palm trees, those in the rear are contained in enormous carved planters. For a Tuscan villa these palms strike a discordant note but pay tribute to the family name.

From 1824 to 1854 the eccentric Mary Farhill was the owner. She left the Villa Palmieri to the grand duchess, Marie Antoinette de Bourbon, who sold it in 1873 to Alexander, earl of Crawford and Balcarres. He shifted the road to Fiesole, which had passed directly in front of his villa and was a halting-transfer spot for stretcher bearers of the Misericordia of Florence and those of Fiesole. To accommodate these charitable men, he built a hospice by the new road, where they could rest and be refreshed (thus the sick were removed from Lord Crawford's terrace view). Most of the gardens really date from the 1870s. In truth, they are fussy and disjointed, lying on a different axis from the villa, and not happily assimilated into a total overall plan.

A high hedge borders a lower parterre garden with a balustraded staircase next to three stately cypresses. A pedestal-fountain with four ground basins is surrounded by four columns canopied with wrought iron. Adjacent to this garden is a pergola leading to a large fishpond/swimming pool. This pool is overhung by a *loggetta* set against an arched wall overgrown with vines, behind which are the tennis courts.

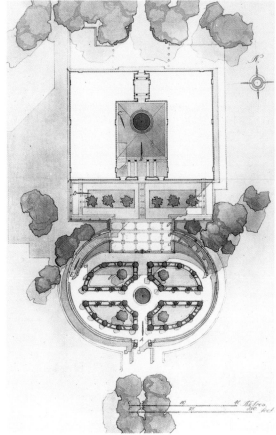

Villa Palmieri, engraving by G. Zocchi (18th century).

Queen Victoria was Lord Crawford's guest at Villa Palmieri first in the spring of 1888, when she planted a cypress which flourishes today, and again in 1893.

In the early twentieth century the gardens and house were carefully restored by James Ellsworth, who also acquired the villetta, partially built in the thirteenth century. This has a small irregular, charming courtyard with brick pavement, a wellhead and ivy-covered walls. A terrace one hundred by twenty feet in front has a formal box garden, rather busy in design. Flowers are grown only in pots set on its walls. To the rear of the villetta is a secret garden with an escalloped wall, and box hedges enclosing flowerbeds. A small octagonal family chapel stands near the villa.

In 1938 Bernon Prentice acquired the villa. More recently it has been enlarged and restored by Castellucci. Presently it is the property of the Bellandi family.

Left:
Villa Palmieri, watercolor by J. C. Shepherd (1925). British Architectural Library, R.I.B.A., London.

Villa Gamberaia

Settignano
Gardens open to the public
when owner not in residence

Villa Gamberaia is a gem in the loveliest of settings. Small and compact, it covers only three acres, but offers great variety, a delicate serenity, and intimacy.

The first mention of the property is in a document dated 17 January 1398 regarding the transfer of ownership of land and a house within the brotherhood of San Martino at Mensola from the abbot to Giovanni di Benozzi. In 1592 Domenico di Jacobo Reccialboni sold the property to Giovanni, a son of the local sculptor Bernardo Rossellino. Because of major renovations it became known as the "Palagio of Gamberaia"—believed to refer to a pond nearby where the peasantry fished for *gambero* (crayfish). In fact, above the door is a shield, of later date, depicting three crayfish on the right-hand side, and two half moons on the left, probably the family crest of the builder of this classic Tuscan villa. A plaque over the door reads "Zanobi Lapi built it in 1610." At his death nine years later, the villa passed to his nephews, Jacopo di Andrea Lapi and Andrea di Cosimo Lapi with the stipulation that at the end of the male line it would eventually be divided between the Capponi and Cerretani families. The nephews set about supplying the property with water, buying up water rights from adjacent neighbors and the farm of La Doccia. They built conduits and large reservoirs. The owners continued to increase the sources of water until 1636, when a lawsuit was brought against them by a neighbor complaining that she was without water because of its removal close to her border. The garden was first laid out between 1624 and 1635. At Andrea's death in 1688, his son Jacopo was forced to heavily mortgage the estate to settle his father's debts. Jacopo's son Giovan Francesco died in 1717 without male heirs, so the Lapi property passed to the Capponi and Cerretani families. During the eighteenth century the garden was updated under Antonio and Piero Capponi, who enlarged the house and added fountains, statues, the grotto garden, and the bowling alley. In 1895 Jeanne Ghyka, princess of Serbia, bought the villa and lived there with an American, Miss Blood. Princess Ghyka was rich, beautiful, and a notorious misanthrope, but she bestowed love upon the garden. She restored the parterre, which had been transformed into vegetable plots, creating the reflecting pools in their place, while retaining the outlines of the beds. The property was subsequently owned by the D'Outrelan family, Baroness Ketteler, Signor Chiesa, and then given to Cardinal Spellman. During World War II the villa was occupied by the German Command, who blew it up upon retreat. The Allies completed the destruction. Fortunately for La Gamberaia, Marcello

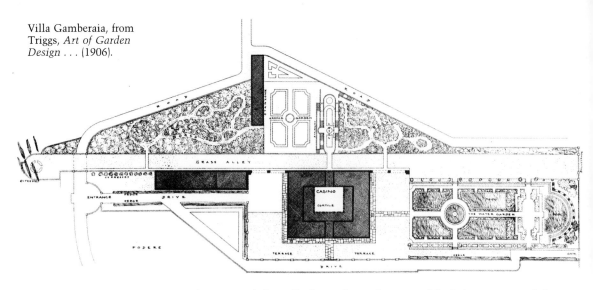

Marchi acquired the villa from the Holy See and had the vision and deter-
mination to rebuild and restore the gardens. It is maintained immaculately
today.

Clipped yews, probably planted by Andrea Lapi, flank the sloping drive
leading to the villa, but it is more evocative to enter the garden from the
gardener's house, which leads into the *limonaia* with the *stanzone*. Borders of peonies and cutting flowers grow in contrast to the dark ilex trees
in the background. This area is a raised terrace connected by a double
staircase with landings to the lower level and to the *bosco.* Here is an
eighteenth-century portion of the garden, a narrow open courtyard with ro-
caille encrustations and pots of hydrangeas. A statue of Pan perches on the
balustrade above the fountain. This opens out onto the bowling green, a
long, lush swath of lawn flanking the villa to the east. One end terminates
at a balcony forming a belvedere over the surrounding olive groves. The
opposite end is lined with potted azaleas and has a shady semicircle carpeted with wildflowers. Benches are set into the rocaille-work wall which
has reliefs of Neptune, sea lions, two musicians, and traces of fountains. A
clump of old cypresses preside over this *nymphaeum.* Above, paths mean-
der through a small *bosco* which traverses the main road. Here wild cyclamen, ivy, and myrtle grow underfoot. To the south of the villa is the parterre, reminiscent of a Persian water garden. The grassy lawn steps gently
down to a slightly sunken level delineated by immaculately clipped, low
hedges, with pebble-patterned paths around the oblong reflecting ponds.
Roses, irises, and lilies grow within the borders. A semicircular pool
backed by arched yew hedges finishes the composition. These hedges were
planted by Princess Ghyka in the late nineteenth century and are now fully mature, framing the view of the Arno River valley beyond.

The villa is rectangular, with a loggia on the first floor overlooking the
water garden. To the west is another long terrace, which looks towards
Florence; its attractive balustrade is topped with statues of dogs entwined
with roses. The villa nestles into its garden, yet looks beyond to the rolling countryside in perfect harmony. The surrounding vineyards and olive
groves do not seem out of keeping next to the strictly ordered parterre.

Boboli

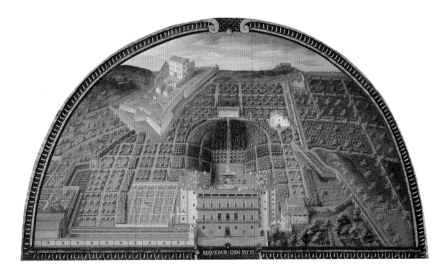

Boboli, lunette by Giusto Utens (1599), Museo Topografico, Florence.

Since the mid-nineteenth century the Renaissance gardens of Boboli have been open to the public, offering a haven from the crowded narrow noisy streets of Florence. The gardens are extensive, spread over hills stretching up to the walls of Fort Belvedere to the southeast, and the city walls of Porta Romana to the south. Occasional performances of the Maggio Musicale Fiorentino in the gardens recall that this garden was built primarily as a backdrop for displays enhancing the Medici dynasty; spaces were allotted for their special interests in botany and zoology, and sport in the form of ball games, equestrian exercises, and bird shooting.

The name Boboli appears to derive from the Borgoli family who owned land on the slopes below Fort Belvedere in the early fifteenth century. Luca Pitti, a rich merchant, began to construct a grandiose palazzo on the site; his letters mention fruit trees on its hillside but no garden. The grand duchess Eleanora, wife of Cosimo de'Medici purchased the unfinished palazzo and land in 1549, adding to it other farms. Cosimo called upon Niccolò Tribolo, who had designed the gardens of Castello ten years before. Tribolo brought water to the garden from Porta San Giorgio, and it is believed that he laid out the basic lines of the garden rising up the hill behind the palazzo. Tribolo died in September 1550 when he was sent to Elba to bring to Florence an enormous block of granite (now forming a basin on the Isolotto). The management of the garden construction passed to Bartolommeo Ammannati who was responsible for the large rusticated courtyard with stairs leading up to the garden, however he was called away on various projects and the job was eventually taken on by Bernardo Buontalenti, a man of great creative talent. The large fantastic grotto is his design. By 1595 the first half of the garden was basically complete. The lunette by Giusto Utens shows the grottoes, fountains, pool, and outline of the amphitheater; many groves and primary paths lead up the hill, converge slightly, and hence add to the sense of perspective. Walking the garden one has the impression that it is much vaster than it actually is. The distances are accentuated by the long straight viales with steep inclines and superb views over the city.

Entering by the Bacchus Gate the visitor is greeted by a fountain of the fat dwarf Morgante, from Cosimo's entourage, posing as a nude Bacchus, seated on a tortoise. Above him is the end of the corridor linking Palazzo Pitti to the Uffizi via Ponte Vecchio. Beyond what was a bowling green is the splendid grotto of Buontalenti. The sober lower portion of the exterior was probably designed by Giorgio Vasari, with niches for Baccio Bandinelli's figures of Adam and Eve, transformed into Apollo and Venus when placed here. Buontalenti's design dates from 1583. The creative and destructive forces of nature are present in this grotto. On the upper part of the facade nature takes over, stalactites and *spugne* ooze out over the thermal window of the cave. Inside is a series of three chambers. The first is a sylvan enchantment of shepherds with their sheep, a metamorphosis of figures emerging out of the *spugne*-surfaced walls. After Michelangelo's death his unfinished slaves were brought here from his studio and placed in the corners where their copies stand today. (The originals are now in the Accademia.) The ceiling is gaily frescoed with wild animals painted by Bernardino Poccetti. Its center originally held a glass fish tank open to the sky, the light casting shimmering patterns on the grotto's floor. The sec-

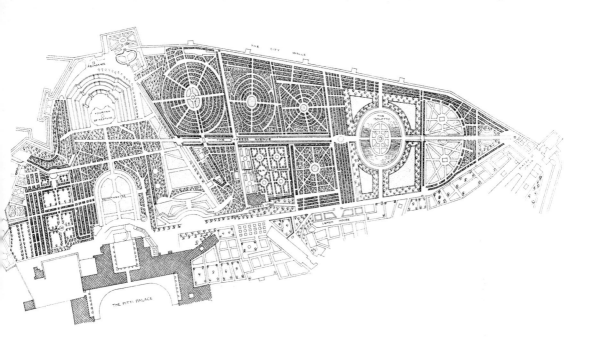

Boboli, from Triggs, *Art of Garden Design . . .* (1906).

ond chamber contains the lusty marble group of Helen and Paris by Vincenzo de'Rossi. The final small, encrusted room has Giambologna's beautiful Venus surprised at her bath by leering figures clutching the rim of the basin. The entire grotto was restored in 1980. A viale leads past the former Garden of Madama—a cutting garden made between 1565 and 1575 for Giovanna of Austria, wife of Francesco I. It originally had columns topped with animals by Ferrucci and a fountain, now replaced by the ungainly figure of Bandinelli's Jupiter, formerly a figure of God the Father, transformed like the Adam and Eve after they were removed from the cathedral's high altar. Close by is the Grotticina di Madama, also restored in recent years. A severe marble door frame is set in the *spugne*. Inside is a small room with marble-patterned floor, *spugne*-covered walls set with geometric molding. At one end emerging from the *spugne* are three life-size naturalistically carved marble goats and a ram's head from which water flows into a large basin below. These delightful figures were carved by Giovanni Fancelli. The grotto built in 1584 is variously attributed to Bandinelli and Tribolo. It predates and influenced Buontalenti's large grotto.

To the rear of the palace is a terrace built above the courtyard's grotto. This terrace has been the site at various times of the Neptune Fountain figure by Stoldo Lorenzi (now in the rectangular pond below Fort Belvedere), then in 1590 for the enormous Juno Fountain complex by Ammannati, originally built for Pratolino, and finally for the Artichoke Fountain by Francesco Susini installed in 1641. Putti sport around the fountain, best seen from a window above; steps spill out from the base of its pool. Beneath it is Ammannati's Moses Grotto with a charming frescoed and garlanded ceiling. The courtyard was used as a theater before construction of the amphitheater. Its most famous fête was the Naumachia of 1589: after a display of processional floats in the garden, including one as a mini-garden complete with birds and topiary, a banquet was held. The guests then adjourned to the courtyard; this had been flooded to a depth of five feet on which a fleet of eighteen Christian galleys attacked a mock Turkish castle. Shortly afterwards the courtyard was drained and ready for dancing. The courtyard had limitations, and the theatrics soon moved completely into the garden. At first, viewing stands were built against the back of the palace, and the action took place against the sloping hillside, the groves and paths serving as backdrops and side entrances. Eventually in 1631 permanent stone walls and tiered seating were built against the hill. The horseshoe-shaped area became the stage, ideal for the elaborately costumed horse ballets—one given in 1637 for the wedding of Ferdinando II and Vittoria della Rovere was on the theme of *Gerusalemme Liberata*, and the theme for the wedding of Prince Cosimo and Margherita Luisa of Orleans in 1661 was *Il Mondo Festeggiante*. Prince Cosimo as Hercules led the troop of horsemen. In the center of the "stage" was a huge statue of Atlas whose globe broke open at the finale to reveal singing young girls representing the four corners of the earth. Twenty thousand spectators viewed this. These elaborate theater pieces ceased with the last Medici, only to be revived in 1933 with the Maggio Musicale's presentation of *A Midsummer Night's Dream*, directed by Max Reinhardt. This was effectively presented on the slopes of the hillside below Fort Belvedere. This area of the Neptune Fountain was originally used for vineyards and orchards. The kaffehaus was built in 1776 by Zanobi del Rosso for the Lorraine dynasty. Just below Fort Belvedere to the south is the casino and garden of the Cavaliere, now used as a porcelain museum. The casino was built as a school house for the last Medici grand duke, Gian Gastone. The garden with its amusing monkey fountain is by Pietro Tacca.

The garden gradually expanded south to Porta Romana. Old walls were torn down, the existing quarries planted over with trees. Alfonso and Giulio Parigi designed this second portion of the garden, with a majestic viale descending to the Isolotto, and continuing the axis through a semicircular meadow with columns and busts, finishing at Porta Romana. The grand viale is lined with ancient cypresses and studded with Greek and Roman statuary from the Medici collection, gravel now takes the place of grass down its center. A gigantic jet of water spurted up before the entrance of the Isolotto. Surrounded by high curving hedges, the large circular fishpond has an island in its center reached by foot bridges. Placed on top of the huge granite basin on the island is the enormous statue of Oceano with crouching rivers. The original Oceano by Giambologna has since been removed to the Bargello. On the island are large pots with citrus trees. Statues of Perseus and Andromeda at opposite sides of the pool strive to be united. Decorative gates are topped with Capricorns, symbols of Cosimo II. Whimsical harpy fountains flank the gates. The Isolotto too served as a stage, in 1948 for Streher's production of *The Tempest*. Set into the hedges of the Isolotto are *pietra serena* (local gray-colored stone) genre statues of great charm. In this newer section of the garden are various fountains and statues depicting buffoons, peasants at their chores and playing rustic games, plus realistic statues of dogs. The areas to either side of the great viale have had various transformations; gone now are the elaborate mazes and thrush traps, dense groves inhabited by cats take their place. Returning up the hill to the palace, one passes the Serraglio built to house small wild animals. Eventually it was transformed into a *limonaia* and served as

Caffehaus, Boboli, engraving by A. Lamberti

a "hospital" for panel paintings soaked during the Florence flood of 1966. Across the lane leading to the Porta d'Annalena are the remains of the Pineapple Garden. Under Cosimo III exotic plants were cultivated here, including the first potatoes to reach Tuscany. In 1841 a forty-seven-page list was published of plant varieties grown in Boboli (excluding fruits). The few flowers found in Boboli today are grown here. Further up the hill by the later addition of the Meridiana wing is a hillside crossed by diagonal paths. When Hitler visited Florence in May 1938, he drove with Mussolini in an open car throughout the gardens; against this hillside were costumed representatives of the historic games of Tuscan cities. During the war that followed, vegetables grew in the gardens and a portion served as a temporary cemetery.

The garden's condition declined with the last Medici and was threatened to be made over in the English style under the early Lorraines. Then, with the Medici return to power in 1814, major attempts were made to restore the garden to its earlier form. On the whole, Boboli is remarkably preserved, thanks to the Soprintendenza dei Monumenti, which maintains and restores it. In recent years many of the more valuable statues have been removed to the Palazzo del Bargello to ensure their preservation.

130 · *Tuscany, Marche*

Villa Palazzina

Siena
Gardens open upon request:
Signor Gianneschi
Strada di Ventena, 28
Siena

The Villa Palazzina, formerly known as Villa Gori, is situated off the road to Vicobello, near the Sienese monastery of the Osservanza.

The garden of the small villa, built in 1620, is characterized by two long ilex tunnels leading off the terrace facing the villa. The pale, buff-colored villa has a voluted roof line and two-storied loggia with the small de'Gori family chapel. Probably in the past there was a formal garden adjacent to the villa on the terrace; however all that remains today is a small stone wellhead with a wrought-iron superstructure. Cypresses have been trained into a pair of arched screens. Behind them are higher terraces with views over the city of Siena and the surrounding countryside.

Lined up with the loggia, running down a gently inclined southern slope is the longer yew tunnel. These hollowed-out, clipped, pleached yews have become gnarled over the centuries, moss and ivy grow up the trunks, and light filters through the branches, providing a shady shelter from the summer heat. On either side are fields of olive trees and wild poppies. The south tunnel leads several hundred yards along a ridge to a knoll and then rises slightly to a solid circular planting of ilex enclosing a bird snare, or *ragnaia*. In the center, bisected by paths, are ilex cut to shrub height in which blinded thrushes were tied, their plaintive songs believed to attract other birds. Hunters could shoot from the sides, remaining hidden. This concept of a birdtrap was often found in Italian villa gardens, but few have been maintained, and this one is much neglected.

Michel de Montaigne described a similar bird snare in the gardens of Benedetto Buonvisi, outside of Lucca (*Montaigne's Journey*, trans. W. Hazlitt, 1859):

> Among other things, I observed several artificial thickets which are very much in fashion about here, and are formed in this way, and for this purpose: upon an elevated piece of ground they plant a diameter of about fifty paces, with all sorts of evergreens, intersected with very narrow covered paths, and surrounded with a small ditch. In the middle of this thicket, there is an open space where the huntsman at a certain time of the year towards November, places himself, provided with a silver whistle, and some tame thrushes, trained for the purpose, and by means of these and birdlime, disposed about in the different little lanes or runs, they sometimes catch 200 thrushes in a single morning. This is only down in a particular district, near the town.

At a right angle to the yew tunnel, a shorter one leads west to a green theater. The stage is raised a few feet above ground level and fronted by a stone wall. The wings were composed of four clipped cypress hedges on either side, with a similar background screen of equal height. To the rear is a single tall cypress tree, placed in the center as if an exclamation point, now obscured by trees growing around it. The audience sits on a raised, horseshoe-shaped ledge, with a flight of graceful steps in the center down to the pit. Behind them is a double ilex hedge which creates an oval corridor for the actors to move about in unobserved. The "orchestra pit" has a lawn crisscrossed by a gravel ribbon path. This remains discernable, but neglected. Maxwell Parrish did a charming illustration of this theater for Edith Wharton's book *Italian Villas and Their Gardens.*

Today the wings of the theater have been replanted in laurel, but the overall effect is ill defined and deserves restoration. It has great delicacy of design.

The yew tunnel returning to the house harbors testimony of the present enjoyment of the garden. A simple rope swing hangs from its branches, and it shelters the doghouse of an elderly Alsatian, Whisky, who accompanied us on our explorations, carrying his favorite pinecone.

It is privately owned by the notary Giovanni Gianneschi.

Green Theater, Villa Palazzina, watercolor by J. C. Shepherd (1925). British Architectural Library, R.I.B.A., London.

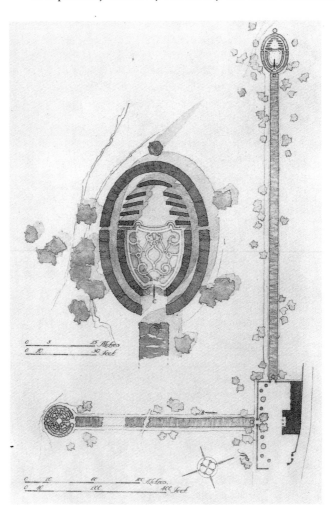

Vicobello

Siena
Gardens open upon request:
Marchesa Chigi-Bonnelli
Via Vicobello, 12
Siena

Vicobello has been a summer residence of the Chigi family since the six-teenth century. Viewed two miles from Siena's northern Porta Ovile, its plan was intended to approximate the shape of the Chigi coat-of-arms. The property is sited on a long ridge which drops off sharply north and south. It is reached by a linden tree avenue. The early sixteenth-century villa is a simple stucco rectangular structure, attributed to Baldassare Peruzzi, paint-er and pupil of the architect Donato Bramante. (Peruzzi's best-known work is the Palazzo Massimi alle Colonne in Rome.) Vicobello is primarily a farming property: the outbuildings are given more prominence than the villa; even the tool shed with its climbing red roses overshadows the cha-pel.

134 · *Tuscany, Marche*

A road parallels the outbuildings, and, as at Centinale, passes between the entrance to the villa's forecourt and a curved gateway set with busts. The gateway leads down to shady rows of cut ilexes, and what was once probably a bowling green, now overgrown, at the base of the hill. The courtyard is reached through a vaulted *porte-cochère.* Inside to the right is a charming well, framed by Ionic columns with urns and the Chigi crest on a pediment.

Through a handsome ivy-covered stone gate set in a high wall to the left of the villa is a formal lemon garden, with large box-edged beds with flowers and gnarled fruit trees. A large luminous lemon *stanzone* continues the line of the outbuildings to the left, opposite is a high hedge of clipped ilex. Within the *stanzone* are the wooden carts to transport the

lemon pots that weigh up to 450 pounds, and require eight men to move them in the first week of November and out the first week of May.

A small, elegant marble summerhouse is opposite the entrance gate. This has a recessed niche with marble benches between two Doric pilasters, surmounted by the Chigi arms, capped with a cardinal's hat. Cypresses in varying heights form a backdrop behind the wall. Passing through a gate set in the hedge one arrives by steep brick steps at a lower terrace with pools, espaliered fruit trees (of which plums predominate), and a circular parterre planted with gray santolina to contrast with the greens. The garden continues down another level to a smaller narrower terrace. Here azaleas and rhododendrons predominate. Hanging under the shady branches of a ginkgo tree are numerous wooden planters containing orchids

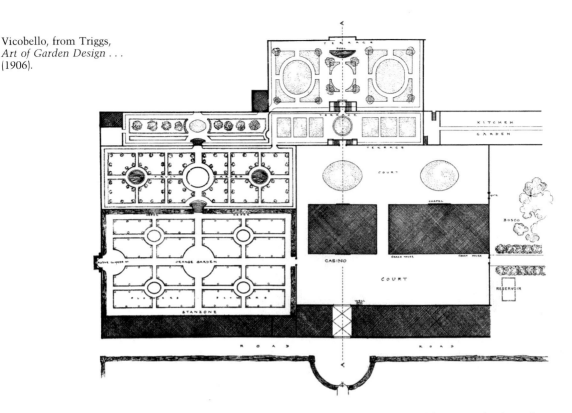

which bloom in mid-August. Palm trees are planted here. At the far right, set at an angle is a *spugne*-textured short tunnel leading into the next garden.

This large rectangular terrace has flower beds, and a large ornamental cedar, a huge ginkgo, a pine tree, more plum trees, and bamboo. A balcony overlooks the olive trees below and Siena in the distance.

Steps lead up to yet another terrace, of the same length, but narrower. Here shaped in box is the Chigi mound, repeated elsewhere in the garden in stone.

The top terrace adjacent to the villa and chapel has oval flower beds with orange trees and lavender. An old English garden bench is inscribed:

Alas that spring should vanish with the rose
That youth's sweet scented manuscript must close
The nightingale that in the branches sang
Ah whence & whither flown again—who knows.

Beyond the terrace to the west is a *bosco*.

In the nineteenth century the Chigi family made some modifications to the villa and the garden. Nothing attributable to Peruzzi remains. Apart from some late additions of stone *spugne* work, the garden architecture details are exquisite, measured in their elegance, nothing superfluous or mean in their ornament.

The marchesa Ginevra Chigi-Bonelli maintains the property beautifully today. Two large white Maremma sheep dogs and a dachshund frolic through the gardens, which are tended by a charming and knowledgeable young gardener. Vicobello is at its best in September, when all the planted beds are blooming.

Castello di Celsa

The Castello di Celsa near Siena features a beautiful view from its garden that was carefully restored after World War II by the late Prince Aldobrandini. His daughter, Livia, now maintains it. The original fortress foundations date back to the thirteenth and fourteenth centuries, when the property was owned by the Celsi family. The castle itself was rebuilt in the early sixteenth century by Mino Celsi, a Lutheran, but the Spanish-Austrian troops left it in ruins in 1554. Inside the castle is a drawing of a project to transform it into a vast Baroque villa. Only the courtyard screen was executed. Much later one tower was extended, and mullioned windows and crenellations were added in the Gothic-revival style. By 1802 the Chigi family owned it, but as described by Joseph Forsyth in his *Remarks* (1816), the castle had a neglected air, with insufficient furniture. Photographs in 1925 show the garden in a pitiful state. It is a joy to compare them to its present condition.

The castle is a three-winged structure with a wedge-shaped courtyard. In the seventeenth century the Baroque triple-arched screen was built linking the towers, and closing off the courtyard. Surprisingly, the result is harmonious. A semicircular stone ramp leads up to the central arch; grillwork covers the apertures. A private road separates this screen from an airy balustraded wall below. At the southeast angle of the castle stands an elegant sober chapel attributed to Baldassare Peruzzi, a leading architect-painter of the High Renaissance. Beneath the wall is a broad parterred terrace ending in a balustraded semicircular pool overlooking the hills towards Siena and Monteriggioni. This view, with groves of olives and oak, has been kept largely intact. The old pleached hedges were probably removed in the mid-seventeenth century. The pool replaces the original fountain, and the Aldobrandini coat-of-arms has altered the earlier geometric parterre patterns, which were very similar to those on a garden design by Peruzzi found in the Uffizi.

Some distance from the castle are the remains on the hillside of the seventeenth-century entrance to the walled *bosco*. This separateness was considered a necessary safety measure against bandits. A villa in this zone of Siena did not have plantings in its immediate vicinity, as this could provide cover to an intruder. The Aldobrandinis have a drawing of the former, very formal state of the *bosco*; the clipped undulating topiary hedges are a more recent addition. A wall with a flight of stairs reaches up to a grilled gate set in a Baroque wall of charming design, alternating sculpted reclining river gods and dolphins, with stretches of balustrades, all capped by

139 · *Castello di Celsa*

urns. Just beyond the gate is a fishpond restored by Prince Aldobrandini. Its rustic stonework is similar to that of Marlia's water theater; in fact, a drawing for the green theater at Marlia exists at the Castello di Celsa with the identical handwriting as that on the Celsa *bosco* design, leading one to believe that the garden architect for both villas was the same. According to the old drawing in the castle, the trees behind the wall were formally clipped like stage wings, radiating from the fishpond, to create an impressive perspective. One central allée remains, but as the years pass this is losing its definition. Wildflowers grow within the walled woodland.

Castello di Celsa, watercolor by J. C. Shepherd (1925). British Architectural Library, R.I.B.A, London.

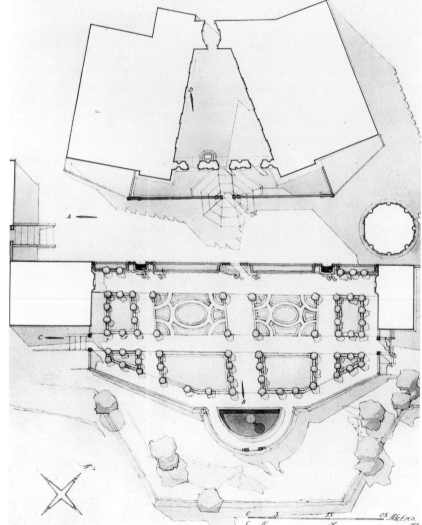

Giardino Buonaccorsi

Potenza Picena
Gardens open upon request:
Signor Renzo Perugini
Società Agripicena
Villa Buonaccorsi
Potenza Picena (Macerata)

Near Potenza Picena is the little-known, but precious Giardino Buonaccorsi. It is one of the very few perfectly preserved gardens in Italy of the eighteenth century, meticulously maintained in its original form by the Buonaccorsi family since its creation. Comparison with an eighteenth-century drawing of the garden showing the upper terraces proves that every detail has been respected; the shape of the beds, the statues, and fountains still are exactly as they were depicted. Although documentation is lacking, the garden has a kinship with the designs of Andrea Vici at Villa Montegallo in Offagna.

The garden consists of five descending terraces behind the villa. These terraces are sheltered by hedges from the breezes, and warmed by the southern exposure. They enjoy a view of the surrounding fields and park and the sea beyond. The three larger terraces increase in size as they descend, each having double rows of flower beds, edged with curving stone borders, as depicted in the fifteenth-century *Hypnerotomachia poliphili* by Francesco Colonna.

At the top level, on the crest of the hill by the villa, is a cleared fore-court. Near it is a gently raised secret garden, within which are star- and diamond-shaped flower beds, centering around little obelisks set on pedes-tals, and surrounded by vases of lemon trees. Statues depicting mythologi-cal figures, putti, and dogs line the central white gravel path, which leads beyond a fountain to a small chapel obscured by tall cypresses. Espaliered on the left wall is a magnificent lemon tree. A Baroque grotto near the vil-la contains a tableau of monks who have been disturbed from their medi-tations by the sudden appearance of a devil emerging from a hidden recess.

In the gravel court before the raised terrace parterre are memorials on marble pedestals to the Buonaccorsi's pet dogs. Topping the wall bordering the side of the villa is a delightful series of comical stone dwarfs dating from the eighteenth century.

The first terrace is raised above the ground-floor level of the villa while the second terrace is level with the ground floor of the villa and linked to the successive lower levels by a staircase edged with figures rep-resenting all the masks of the Commedia dell'Arte. Additionally, this ter-race is connected to the upper raised terrace by a pergola, riddled with *giochi d'acqua*. Presiding over this level is a large statue of Flora against the eastern wall. She is also equipped with concealed water jets. The free-standing statues of Roman emperors were once set in topiary niches, now the hedges are low, narrowing the terrace to appear like a corridor.

The third terrace has an abundance of flowering plants, changed ac-cording to the season, in parterres of geometrical shapes. It is less stiffly conceived than the parterres of the upper levels. This level and the following terrace may have been later additions. Again, obelisks and an espaliered lemon tree are featured. On the eastern wall is the entrance to the *bosco*.

The lowest terrace features square flower beds, with tall hedges dividing the paths set with ornaments and brick fountains. The garden ends against a high wall, masked with greenery. Set in this wall facing the central staircase is a chamber decorated with tufa and pebbles. It has ingenious polychrome moving figures whose eighteenth-century mechanisms still function. There is a miniature forge, a huntsman, and musicians wearing the costumes of a Turk and a Harlequin. The mechanical grottoes of Pratolino and the Fountain of the Owl at Tivoli are lost to us, hence the maintenance of these moving figures with their *giochi d'acqua* is all the more important for Italian garden history.

The ornamental park, or *bosco*, was created in the nineteenth century in the English fashion. It features a small artificial lake, and a mount for viewing the countryside. The meandering path leads up to two small enclosed garden rooms flanking the octagonal chapel. These enclosures are planted with a palm tree and succulents.

Since the death of the countess Giuseppina Buonaccorsi, the garden has been under the direction of the Società Agripicena. The villa itself is used as a restaurant, the park as a setting for concerts and theatrical productions. The tiny Buonaccorsi chapel is often used for weddings, with the receptions held in the gardens. Fortunately the Società Agripicena is determined to maintain the garden unaltered.

III *Latium* *Campania*

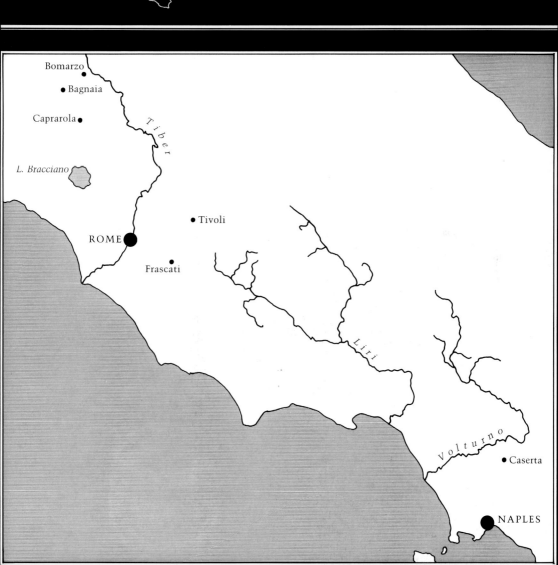

Bomarzo

Bagnaia

Caprarola

Tiber

L. Bracciano

Tivoli

ROME

Frascati

Liri

Volturno

Caserta

NAPLES

Villa Lante

Bagnaia
Gardens open to the public
(closed Mondays)

This small garden is perfection, full of gently murmuring water and shifting shadows, silvery greens, and mellowed stone carved with great taste and delicacy. The special appeal of this Renaissance garden is its intimate link with nature—the *bosco* of ancient plane trees melds freely with the architectural garden elements in contrast to the geometrically designed *quadrato* below. Light filters through the branches shading the four successive terraces rising on the hillside. The trees part for the passage of water, which winds its way down towards the *quadrato.* From the top of the hill, water flows down cascades to a water-chain, across a channel cut in a banquet table, then over a retaining wall, splashing figures of reclining giants, and surfacing again in the guise of multiple candles in the concave fountain above the *quadrato.* The water ends in the central square lake, crossed by footpaths, with a circular basin and fountain in the center, surmounted by the famous four moors holding up the *monte* emblem of the Montalto family. Nothing is out of scale or crude. A perfect Renaissance garden—all is to the measure of man and subordinate to the garden as a whole. The twin villas are placed to frame the view of the garden rising up the hillside. They do not compete for attention with the other elements, but complement them, yet the design of the villas is stately in its detail and by a master architect, with all probability, Giacomo Barozzi da Vignola.

Although there is no surviving documentation, logic points to Vignola as author of the garden plan and designer of the paired villas. He worked extensively in the area of Viterbo, creating private villas, including his masterpiece Villa Farnese, twenty miles from here at Caprarola. The water-chain at Villa Lante is very similar to that of Caprarola, where it is composed of shrimp-like forms, here of simple volutes. This and the garden's spatial treatment can be considered trademarks of Vignola. Cardinal Gambara, who commissioned the garden, had undoubtedly visited Caprarola and Tivoli's Villa d'Este. A man with a deep affinity to nature, he desired a garden on a more intimate scale, featuring the play of water as at Tivoli, yet stressing interplay of the woods and garden, barely hinted at around the casino of Caprarola. Indeed this is the first Renaissance garden in which the *bosco*, formerly present as an adjacent, but separate garden element, is fully integrated into the garden itself. The garden proper is composed of the *quadrato*, or square flat parterre area covering about an acre beneath the twin villas, with a square lake in the center; a pair of *rampes-douces* with flanking steps between the villas brings you to the first

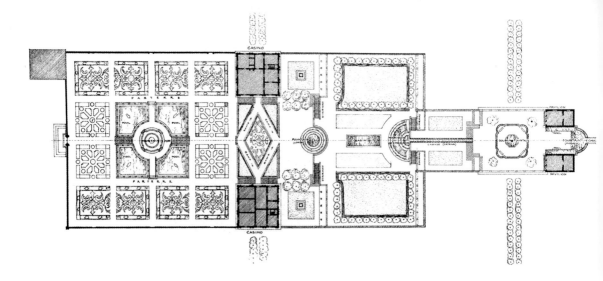

of four terraces ascending the hillside. (The slope is fifty feet high.) The
top two terraces are somewhat narrower than the preceding ones. Here the
woods intermingle: light filters through the leaves of ancient plane trees
and ilex on clearings set with fountains and stone benches. Beyond the
walled-in garden is an informal park, formerly a hunting preserve now reduced in size, traversed by long straight paths with occasional fountains at
junctions and a maze.

The small town of Bagnaia nestles at the foot of the garden. It was the
fief of the bishopric of Viterbo, and the Villa Lante was lent as a summer
retreat to the cardinals who held the bishopric—usually nephews of the
current pope. In the fourteenth century, the bishopric of Viterbo produced
little income; to augment it, the town and lands of Bagnaia were added to
its territory. In the late fifteenth century the Bishop of Viterbo, Raffaele
Sansone Riario, often hunted on the wooded slopes of Monte Cimini. He
put up the first building here in 1477. His nephew, Ottavio Riario, enclosed the property as a hunting preserve, and erected the hunting pavilion, which still stands today in the park. The Medici pope Leo X came
here to hunt as his guest, and passed the bishopric on to his nephew Cardinal Niccolò Ridolfi who made improvements including conveying water
to the property by means of a large aqueduct fed by two springs.

The brother of Pope Julius III, Cardinal Balduino del Monte, held it
until Pope Pius V, in the name of the Apostolic Camera, gave the property
to Cardinal Giovanni Franscesco Gambara who became bishop in 1566. He
had plans drawn up for the gardens as we know them today. Pope Gregory
XIII, hearing the praises of the garden, announced his intended visit. Gambara pushed ahead construction, finishing the first villa (to the left), and
adorned his buildings with the family crest of the crayfish, or *gambero*.
The pope was unable to come in person, and sent the dour San Carlo Borromeo in his place in 1580. His inspection provoked sharp criticism of
Gambara's extravagance, which could, he thought, have been much better
directed at a hospital for the poor of Viterbo. Cowed by this, Gambara did
not dare to build the projected twin villa, but spent the money saved on it
for a hospital and embellished the local cathedral. He loved his gardens

passionately, "my delight" as he called them. Michel de Montaigne visited the following year, writing (*Montaigne's Journey*, trans. W. Hazlitt, 1859):

> Saturday, 30th of September, I left Viterbo early in the morning, and took the road to Bagnaia, a country-seat belonging to Cardinal Gambara, one of the most richly ornamented places I ever saw. It is so well provided with fountains, that in this respect it not only equals, but surpasses, both Pratolino and Tivoli. . . . When the decorations here are completed, it will be the finest place of the sort in the world. One of the most remarkable features is a pyramid which spouts forth water in different directions; at each base of this pyramid, is a small lake, full of pure and limpid water. In the center of each lake is a stone boat, wherein stand two figures, in the costume of crossbowmen, who, through their cross-bows, shoot continuous streams of water against the pyramid. The grounds are traversed by a number of well-planned walks, with carved stone seats at short distances. The palace is small, but well arranged. The cardinal was not at home; but, as he is French at heart, his people received us with the utmost kindness.

Despite continued pressures to turn the property over to the Holy See, Gambara resisted. In 1587 his successor, Cardinal Casale, purchased it for the bishopric of Viterbo and bequeathed it to the Holy See. That same year Pope Sixtus gave it to his nephew, the youthful Cardinal Alessandro Peretti Montalto. Montalto took up where Gambara left off, building the second villa—the first was primarily a residence for the owner, the second had a reception hall and guest rooms. He built additional fountains and transformed the central fountain in the *quadrato* described by Montaigne. The pyramid was substituted by the group of four delightful moors holding up his family emblem of the *monte* and the star. These statues are variously ascribed to Giambologna and Taddeo Landini. They appear to be of bronze but are actually of travertine, hardened and darkened by sunlight and the water, which rises in jets beneath their feet. Antonio Canova, tapping the statues with his hammer commented, "It will outlast marble." Indeed the mellow aging of the stonework in the garden is one of its happiest features.

Montalto entertained here many of the famous personalities of his day; Connestàbile Marcantonio Colonna, the duke of Mantua, Duke Cesare d'Este, and Pope Clement VIII, who fostered the creation of the Aldobrandini garden at Frascati after visiting Villa Lante. A contemporary chronicle tells how he passed an afternoon here dining, resting, and touring the gardens, then world famous for the quantity of fresh clear waters, and for the variety and size of its fountains.

The gardens then passed to papal nephews, Cardinal Ludovico Ludovisi, Antonio Barberini, and Federico Sforza.

After the Lante villa on the Janiculum hill was pulled down to make way for city fortifications, the family requested the property at Bagnaia in compensation. This was not fully granted for three generations. In the meantime Pope Alexander VII gave Duke Ippolito Lante a long lease with a minimal payment annually of six scudi. It was renewed a century later under Benedict XIV, and finally, in the middle of the nineteenth century Pius IX granted them title to the entire property. The Lantes used the villa as a summer residence for three hundred years until World War II. Fortunately, the Lantes respected the original garden design, modifying only the parterres and the hedge-shape in the *quadrato*. In 1685 the duchess of Lante, Louise Angelique de la Tremoille, brought in a French gardener who combined the six side parterres as seen in a print of 1614 into four, created

the *broderie* pattern, and clipped the bordering hedges of box in the French style. Having done this he mysteriously drowned in the Fountain of the Moors.

Louise Angelique was the pretty young wife of the much older duke, and loved lighthearted diversions. With her famous sister, Princess des Ursins, she filled the gardens with guests such as the ambassador Cardinal d'Estrées who was entertained with music, comedy, and rope dancing.

In 1757 the Scottish architect Robert Adam came and made a drawing of the Fountain of the Moors. Fifteen years later Cardinal Marcello Lante revised the entrance and added the wrought-iron gate. Its last era of brilliance was under the duchess Margherita Marescotti, wife of Don Vincenzo Lante, a Florentine hostess who attracted gifted amateurs for her theatricals in 1820.

In the middle of the *quadrato* is a square lake, crossed by four footpaths joining and circling its central basin and the Fountain of the Moors. In the four compartments of the lake are the stone boats described by Montaigne, now occupied by putti and flowers. The Lante eagle surmounts the north gate. Camellias, hortensias, citrus, and azaleas flourish here. Old photographs of the *rampes-douces* show the triangular central area planted with box spelling out "Villa Lante." The flanking steps are riddled with surprise water jets. At the first terrace is a concave tiered fountain with multiple water jets, the so-called candle fountain—each vertical jet set on the ledge resembles a candlestick; alternately jets on the sides of the walls spurt water. This fountain recalls the Path of the One Hundred Fountains at Tivoli. Urns carved with small masks top the balustrade. Above this fountain is an excellent view of the parterre *quadrato*.

The second terrace features the long stone table with water flowing through the channel cut across its length, designed after Pliny's description of an Imperial garden table designed to cool wine and fruit. Grassy lawns and shady plane trees make this spot inviting. A large convex basin stands at the end, with well carved, reclining river gods, holding cornucopias by the steps. Water cascades down the center over two cups. This is fed from the charming water-chain on the third terrace. This slim canal cascade is composed of volutes. Hedges border it and lead you up a flight of steps to the fourth terrace. Appearing here according to a 1614 print was a fantastic pavilion which perhaps was never built. Today the Fountain of the Dolphins takes its place. This is a tiered, octagonal fountain with water spouting from the mouths of dolphins and lion masks. Stone benches under the plane trees surround the fountain. At the end of the garden are graceful twin porticoed pavilions—"Rooms of the Muses"—flanking a grotto with water gushing from above, affording a cool retreat from the sun-swamped *quadrato*. Rows of Doric columns enclose this area. The grotto is completely covered by moss and ferns and is backed by high trees. This is the source of water for the garden, in the park its final destination is a large oval fishpond backed by a high balustraded retaining wall. Pegasus prances in the water surrounded by water nymphs, and watched over by female busts set on large consoles.

The Lante family continued to summer here until 1932 when they then abandoned the villa. It suffered from bombs and successive waves of occupying troops. In 1953 Angelo Cantoni purchased the villa and established the Società Villa Lante to restore and preserve the gardens. The villa and gardens are now open to the public, magnificently renewed and maintained.

Sacro Bosco

Bomarzo
Gardens open to the public

Ideally, the Sacred Wood of Bomarzo should be first seen on a misty morning. The bizarre, enormous statues would then loom out of the fog, appearing even more mysterious, and imparting the same feeling of discovery of those who began excavating the gardens after centuries of abandonment.

The entire garden is puzzling, and unlike any other. Enigmatic inscriptions are engraved on the soft tufa stone sculptures hinting at the meanings of these wild figures and guiding the visitor forward. This is not a garden in a conventional sense. It is placed at considerable distance from the residence, in a gully below the hill town of Bomarzo. One must traverse a stream to enter into the woods. Do not expect flower beds or specimen trees, formal paths or fountains set in box parterres. The path meanders under shady trees, emerges in a sheep pasture, and retreats again to finish at a grove. Its appeal lies in the journey into the eccentric mind of its creator, Pier Francesco Orsini, known as Vicino, duke of Bomarzo.

Vicino Orsini was an attractive, cultivated man of letters, yet also a soldier. Connected by family ties to King Henri II, he fought on the French side in the Flemish wars. At the defeat of the French at Hesdin by the Spanish in 1553, he was imprisoned for two years.

After his release, Vicino continued his military career defending Tivoli against the Spanish, and fought at Velletri and Monte Fortino. Late in 1556 peace was concluded, and he was able to return to his beloved Bomarzo. By 1563, although not completed, the garden was well known in the area. Torquato Conti was approached by Annibale Caro, owner of the Villa Catena at Poli, for suggestions for fresco themes to rival those marvels of the Sacro Bosco. To our knowledge, an allegorical garden with such autobiographical references—Vicino as warrior, the Orsini bears, the temple to Giulia—was not imitated on so extensive a scale elsewhere. Bomarzo remains unique in its genre.

Dating the garden is difficult. Giulia Farnese probably died in 1546, an inscription on the *tempietto* gives this date. The pedestal by the *nymphaeum* is inscribed "1552" with the name of Vicino as creator, so we can guess that this was its commencement date. He was away from Bomarzo between 1553 and 1557. After this he returned to make the villa his residence for the remainder of his life. From the ongoing references to the garden in his letters we can assume it was developed until his death in 1585.

Various sculptors and architects have been suggested as possibly re-

sponsible for the Sacro Bosco. Among them, Giacomo Barozzi da Vignola, Jacopo del Duca, Bartolommeo Ammannati, and Pirro Ligorio. Without a doubt Vicino himself conducted the program of the sculptures as well as the choice of inscriptions. He was very well read, with personal contacts among the leading poets of the day, and had traveled extensively throughout Europe. Among the inscriptions are clues to his purpose: at the beginning a base advises that "You who wander through the world to see its stupendous marvels, come here, where there are horrible faces, elephants, lions, monsters, and dragons," and again, "Who with raised eyebrows and tight lips avoids this place, fails to admire the seven wonders of the world." There is a shift of mood from the lower portion of the garden hidden in deep shade, populated by sensuous female figures and ferocious monsters and giants to the higher, open sunnier portion where the three-headed dog of Cerberus marks its approach. On the edge of a meadow stands the *tempietto* in memory of Giulia Farnese. Here we are on a more spiritual plane.

The other zones of the garden have a strong current of metamorphosis. Ovid's tales were very familiar to the Renaissance mind, and no doubt inspired the sculptures. Forms emerge out of the rock and struggle forth from the earth, such as the sleeping nymph, the Aphrodite or Amphitrite, and the whale.

There is a strong sense of the primeval, of creation, decay, and menace. A standing giant tears apart the limbs of his fellow held upside down—a reference to Ludovico Ariosto's *Orlando Furioso*. An oriental dragon is attacked by dogs. Nearby stands an elephant crushing a Roman soldier in its trunk, possibly referring to the Battle of Hesdin, where the opposition's general had a coat-of-arms containing an elephant. Enormous masks with gaping mouths swallow up the visitor who passes through them. One is a garden house, with a table and seats within the mouth. An inscription rings the mouth, "Ogni pensiero vola" (or "Every thought flies"

Interspersed with the statues are architectural features, such as the remains of the *nymphaeum*, and a two-storied tower, which slipped to a precarious tilt during an earthquake, adding to its charm. At various levels there are grassy terraces—one has rows of over-size vases, the other is bordered by enormous pinecones and acorns, the Orsini rampant bear supporting a gigantic rosette stands guard at one end.

The theme of water plays a prominent part. A stream sets apart the *bosco*. Excavations have revealed a complex system of conduits. Figures of Neptune, fish-tailed sirens, a whale, and a turtle populate the Sacro Bosco. The Fountain of Pegasus alludes to Monte Helicon, sacred to Apollo, where Pegasus' striking hoof created a spring. Thus Vicino Orsini's links to the intellectual world are honored.

Yet tempting as it is to find a coherent pattern linking the garden together, one must not overlook Vicino's admonitions inscribed on pedestals: "Sol per sfogar il cor" ("Only for the heart's amusement"), and "Dimmi poi se tante meraviglie sien fatte per inganno o per arte." A sphinx sits over the latter inscription inviting us to ponder whether the statues were made by trickery or by art. Vicino had the statues painted brightly, which must have enhanced their sense of surreality to the visitor of the sixteenth century.

The guiding inscriptions were probably inspired by the descriptions in Francesco Colonna's *Hypnerotomachia*, whose lover Poliphilus wandered lost in a garden. A number of the statues had classical prototypes—the river god, the sphinx, the Cerberus, and the enlarged theatrical masks, as well as the architectural style of the *tempietto*. Yet these works are all exaggerated and distorted in the Mannerist style of their day.

After the death of Duke Vicino, the subsequent owners of Bomarzo let it fall into an abandoned state. Legends evolved of a hunchbacked Duke Vicino, who was at odds with his father and brothers. Supposedly his wife was seduced by his younger brother, who was then killed by a vengeful Vicino. The Sacro Bosco was believed to conceal a family scandal, and hence was deliberately neglected. Even today, superstitious Italians avoid the *bosco*, considering it an evil place. It is said that certain Orsini family papers are held back from scholars. Manuel Mujica-Lainez wrote a novel, *Bomarzo*, exploring the moody character of Duke Vicino, who was also the inspiration for a banned opera by Alberto Ginastera. In all probability the reasons for the garden's abandonment were far more prosaic. Vicino's heirs simply did not share his personal vision and obsession for the Sacro Bosco. The fief of Bomarzo was sold to the Lante family in 1645, and subsequently passed to the Borghese family. The garden was purchased by Giovanni Bettini, who recently directed its restoration and opened it to the public.

Villa Farnese

Caprarola
Gardens open upon request:
Soprintendenza per i
beni ambientali e ar-
chitettonici del Lazio
Via Cavaletti, 2
Rome

Teatro dietro al Palazzino, al quinto Piano del Giardino di Caprarola

Villa Farnese, engraving by J. P. Pantnus from L. Dami, *Il Giardino Italiano* (1924).

Villa Farnese reveals itself stage by stage, reserving the best for last. One approaches the palazzo through the narrow main street of the small hill town, suddenly coming upon a sloping elliptical piazza, ramps leading to a larger trapezoidal court, with succeeding double staircases to massive bastions forming the bottom portion of the palazzo. Dominating the entire town, the palazzo incorporates the base of a fortress built by the Florentine Antonio da Sangallo the Younger. It should be remembered that before the seventeenth century to the south of Rome it was not the custom to have country houses with gardens, as they were considered vulnerable to brigand attacks. Thus here, behind the palazzo the garden-park is set off by a moat and the entire area is enclosed by high walls running almost three miles.

Its creator, Cardinal Alessandro Farnese II, had serious doubts about choosing Caprarola for his residence. As his letters (to Monsignor Archinto and Margaret of Austria) written in 1555 testify, he would have preferred family properties either in Frascati, which was a more civilized town, with

157 · *Villa Farnese*

the added attractions of possible archaeological excavations, or the Villa Madama, just outside of Rome. Caprarola belonged from about 1200 to the Orsini family until it was bought by the first Cardinal Farnese who built the fortress. In 1550 Cardinal Alessandro II purchased the adjacent hillside and hired Giacomo Barozzi da Vignola as architect. The outcome is Vignola's masterpiece. Jakob Christopher Burckhardt, writing of it in *The Civilization of the Renaissance in Italy* (1860), calls it ". . . perhaps the highest example of restrained majesty which secular architecture has achieved."

The family fortunes were cemented by Giulia Farnese Orsini, the favorite of the Borgia pope Alexander VI. Under her influence, Pope Alexander made her brother Alessandro the first Farnese cardinal. He in time became Pope Paul III and in turn created his grandson Alessandro II cardinal at the age of fourteen, endowing him with rich archbishoprics, including that of Avignon. This second Cardinal Alessandro was a much respected patron of the arts. To Caprarola came Giorgio Vasari, Baldassare Castiglione, and Cardinal Bembo. A Renaissance prince of the Church was expected to live lavishly. Even so, San Carlo Borromeo, who controlled the purse strings of the cardinals, protested at the soaring costs of the construction of Caprarola, saying that such expenses would be better used to relieve the poor. Cardinal Alessandro responded, "Ma io il denaro l'ho dato ai poveri, poco a poco, facendoglielo guadagnare con il loro sudore." ("But I have given the money to the poor, little by little, making them earn it with their sweat.") His letters reflect his deep interest in the garden, extending down to selection of the fountains.

After Alessandro's death in 1587 the palazzo passed to his nephew Odoardo. Inventories prove it was practically complete at that date. It stayed in the Farnese family until 1731 when the line died out. Then by inheritance it passed to the Bourbon Carlo III of Spain, later of Naples. At this time the library and art collection were removed to Naples and a period of abandonment ensued. From 1750 the palazzo was neglected and unlived in for one hundred years. One caretaker ripped out and sold ninety thousand pounds of lead fountain piping and disposed of much of the remaining furniture and timber. No restorations were carried out until after 1870 when the last two tenants made efforts to restore the gardens, but photographs at the turn of the century and descriptions by Edith Wharton clearly show the state of decay and crumbling of statues and walls. Fortunately the state purchased Villa Farnese in 1940, and since 1948 the casino, formerly tenanted by peasants whose children begged from visitors, has become a pristine summer residence of the President of the Republic. The palazzo is now open to the public, but the casino, set back in the park, can only be visited by special permit. Today, just as Charles Latham related in 1905 in *The Gardens of Italy*, "the place is guarded as if every tourist were a conspirator in disguise. The custodian, it may be added, is absolutely incorruptible."

The palazzo is in the shape of a pentagon. Vignola added two stories above the bastions. The resulting mass is imposing from the piazza below. The approach today is free from traffic; without much difficulty one can imagine sixteenth-century soldiers loitering on the ramps and piazzas, the large expanses scorching in the summer sun, windswept in the blustery

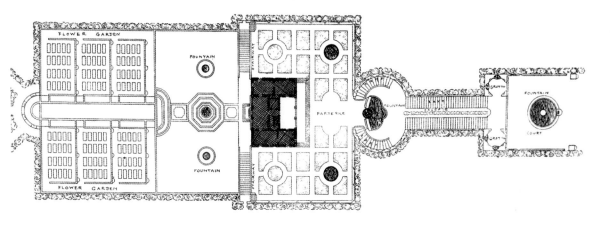

winter. Within the palazzo is a circular courtyard and extraordinary staircase with endless frescoed rooms by the Zuccari family. The effect is over-
whelmingly formal. To the rear, looking out from the piano nobile rooms,
are two formal square terrace gardens echoing the angled walls of the palazzo yet separated from it by a dry moat. These gardens date from 1557
and have fountains set in broad cross paths with quartered parterres. Because of the positioning of these two terraces, one used in the cooler
months, is gathering the sun from the south. The other is protected from
the blazing summer sun by the shade of a projecting wall. Ten cypresses
were planted between pairs of statues representing the seasons. About half
of the trees survive, enormous with age. Set between diagonal angles of
these two terraces is a much smaller garden which links the two larger
ones. It was probably conceived of as a *giardino segreto*. Odoardo Farnese
lived at Caprarola almost year-round, and favored this small garden, planting it with roses. Today camellias abound. Two large caryatids guard the
wooded area beyond and a grotto harbors figures of shepherds. Michel de
Montaigne in 1580 visited and wrote (*Montaigne's Journey*, trans. W. Hazlitt, 1859), "In the grounds, also, there are several things well worth
seeing, and among others, a grotto, where the water showering out into a
small lake, gives to the eye a close imitation of the fall of real rain." He
found the site "sterile and alpine," but the garden still had much work to
transform it further.

Beyond the terraces is a vast park of scotch firs, umbrella pines, ilexes,
huge holm oaks, chestnuts, and ancient beeches. Four hundred firs were
transplanted from the mountains of Camaldoli for Cardinal Alessandro II.
Across the park, a long avenue of larches widens suddenly and surrounds a
round fountain set in the turf. Thus one comes upon the delightful *giardino grande*, with hills rising up behind a small casino. In mood and physi-
cal distance from the palazzo this garden constitutes a true retreat from
formality.

Built into a gentle slope is the delicate casino, also by Vignola, consisting of one story on the lower front side, with two in the back, a slender columned loggia set on a terrace surrounded by low walls with clipped box parterres, and three identical horse motif fountains. This is presided over by twenty-eight humorous Renaissance marble *canephori,* or basket/urn-bearing figures, unique of their sort and utterly charming. The ladies support urns on their heads; the bearded men similarly balance baskets. One figure drinks from a wineskin, another blows a conch shell towards his companion who covers her ears, one lady caresses her breasts, another figure holds young birds or grapes. A nymph clasps her hands behind her head and appears to relax in the peace of the garden. They set the tone for the cardinal's private entertainments held here; for example a masque in honor of Pope Gregory XIII's visit in 1585 with participants parading in white costumes carrying olive branches and sounding cymbals. One can imagine meals here on hot summer days with the relief of the wind through the dark cypresses and umbrella pines, the songs of birds, and the murmur of the water in the multitude of fountains.

In front of the casino is a staircase graced by horses and dolphins. As a focal point, two hoary water gods wearily supporting trickling cornucopias recline between a chalice fountain with water splashing down to a lichen-covered basin, and hence bubbling down a cascade edged with carved curving dolphins, to finish in a shell, all flanked by grassy steps and retaining walls. This is an elaboration on Villa Lante's cascade.

Behind the casino, reached by either of the two staircases ornamented with dolphins, and to the rear of the parterre, are three further balustraded terraces. These create extension rooms of the casino itself. Originally planted with small fruit trees, the garden was redesigned with twenty small flowerbeds in each section, comprising a total of 120 subdivisions. This ambitious layout has been abandoned now. Eighteen mask wall-fountains trickle water into wall basins. Pebble pavements surround flower beds that depict the Farnese lily and peacock. In the foreground is a pool with a gilt fountain in the center and the Farnese lily. The garden terminates in a semicircular walled area where nymphs riding horses perch on top of pilasters and three freestanding fountain gates topped by urns and globes lead back into the woods.

Seen from the air, the palazzo's park melds into the surrounding wooded hillside, with Monte Soracete and the Comincini hills in the far distance. This is a Renaissance garden still, with sharply defined garden spaces; the wilderness is apart from the formal elements.

Of the many guests to Caprarola, perhaps it was most appreciated by the former Cardinal Camillo Pamphili and his wife Olympia, the beautiful young widow of Prince Borghese. With great difficulty the cardinal obtained from Pope Innocent X release from his vows arguing that he could "practice the virtue of chastity better with a wife." He discreetly wed Olympia in 1647. To avoid scandal they quietly took up residence in remote Caprarola, enjoying the peace and beauty of its gardens so much that when it was time to leave and move on to what is now the priory of the Order of Malta in Rome, they transplanted to its garden many flowers from Caprarola.

163 · *Villa Farnese*

Villa Madama

Rome
Gardens open upon request:
Ufficio Informazioni
Ministero degli Affari Esteri
Via Collegio Romano, 27
Rome

Villa Madama was the first great Roman suburban villa of the Renaissance. Few traces of the proposed garden and only half of the proposed villa remain today. Much of the garden layout is based on conjecture, but it cannot be dismissed in a survey of Italian Renaissance gardens, for it was highly influential throughout Italy. It is tantalizing to imagine how it would have been complete. Although vast in scale, letters and a few drawings give us enough to realize that it was conceived with great simplicity and breadth of design, resulting in the most perfect interpenetration of villa and garden.

The property is on the eastern slope of Monte Mario, with views from its terrace of the Tiber and the *campagna*. Raphael created a master plan for Cardinal Giuliano de'Medici; much of the execution appears to have been done by his friend and pupil, Giulio Romano. Antonio da Sangallo the Younger and his family had a hand in the garden design. Giovanni da Udine contributed delicate grotesque designs and at least one fountain.

Although the construction was well underway by 1516, there were serious setbacks. With the death of Cardinal Giuliano's uncle, Pope Leo X, in December 1521, funds were cut and work halted. Raphael died in 1520 and there were squabbles between Giulio Romano and Giovanni da Udine. Cardinal Medici had become Pope Clement VII and could devote less time to supervising personally the development of the villa. In desperation he assigned Bishop Mario Maffei of Volterra the unenviable task of mediator between the quarreling artists. The completed portion of the villa became, like the Villa Farnesina, a pavilion for entertaining, not a residence. The last major fête before the Spanish sack of Rome in 1527 was held in honor of Isabella d'Este. Pope Clement VII stood helplessly on the ramparts of Castel Sant'Angelo watching the troops of Pompeo Colonna burn his villa. Afterwards he tried to rebuild it, but the project lost momentum. The property passed to the Order of Sant'Eustace until around 1537 when it was bought by the widow of Duke Alessandro de'Medici, Emperor Charles V's illegitimate daughter Margherita. From her, the Villa Madama takes its name. She lived there until her remarriage to Ottavio Farnese when she became the duchess of Parma. Then the villa was neglected. In the summer of 1555 Cardinal Alessandro Farnese wrote to her asking if he might rent the property and improve it, but she refused, and he turned instead to Caprarola. Through Margherita's daughter the villa passed to the Bourbon rulers of Naples in 1755. Utter neglect set in. The property remained in the Bourbon family into the twentieth century. It became overgrown, but was appreciated by the Romantics, among them Goethe, who visited to meditate on the verdant ruins and enjoy the magnificent views.

At the beginning of the eighteenth century some attempt was probably made to restore it, but the real restoration had to wait until the beginning of this century when M. Bergès hired the architect Piò Piacentini to complete the walled walks, guided by the original design of Antonio da Sangallo. Count Dentice became the next owner, until it was purchased in the 1960s by the Italian State to be used as headquarters of the Presidenza del Consiglio dei Ministri. Some restoration work of the gardens has been undertaken. Today it can only be visited by permission.

The sources for the garden were found in Imperial Rome, where patrician gardens had been constructed on the slopes of the Palatine. The scale of Villa Madama was inspired by the monuments of ancient Rome. Ruins were studied—specifically, the Temple of Neptune at the Imperial palaces, and possibly a *nymphaeum* which was part of Nero's Golden House. In turn the villa's garden was famed throughout Italy and inspired most subsequent gardens of the sixteenth century. Duke Francesco Maria of Urbino borrowed a letter from Baldassare Castiglione by Raphael describing this project which was then used by the architect Bartolommeo Genga to serve as inspiration for Villa Imperiale at Pesaro, built around 1522. After Spanish Imperial forces sacked Rome in 1527, the painter Perino del Vaga fled to Genoa where elements of Villa Madama appear in Palazzo Doria's garden loggia. In turn, Giulio Romano went to Mantua where his work on Palazzo del Tè reflects this garden. The concept of interpenetration of villa and garden was perhaps its most lasting contribution, along with the successive panoramic garden rooms, and its site against the hillside.

Approaching the villa from the southeast are semicircular steps between two round towers. A third tower is at the northeast corner of the loggia's adjacent garden room.

The original plans envisioned a rectangular courtyard with adjacent rectangular garden. On this axis of the entrance was then to have been a staircase leading into the villa itself, with a large circular central court-

Fishpond, Villa Madama, from G. Vasi, *Magnificenze di Roma* (1747–59).

yard. Only half of this courtyard was built, as can be seen in Vasi's mid-eighteenth-century print, with alternating windows framed by small Ionic columns between set-in rounded columns. Continuing on this north-south axis, the villa ends in a magnificent vaulted loggia with delicate stucco and fresco grotesques by Giovanni da Udine and Romano, inspired by the excavations taking place on the Palatine at the time. Originally the loggia opened up with triple arches onto a garden room, walled on three sides, which was conceived as a natural extension of the lofty loggia. To protect the decoration of the loggia these arches are now bricked up. The garden room, known as the Piazzale della Fontana, was planted with trees, box parterres, and has two niches for statuary and a fountain. Giovanni's Fountain of the Elephant remains here today. Though in poor condition, it is the last of the important pieces of garden architecture to survive. The sarcophagus, with putti to catch the water issuing from the trunk of the elephant's head, is now gone. According to Giorgio Vasari this elephant motif with its mosaics, personal emblem of Cardinal Giuliano, and garland of flowers and fruit was inspired by the Temple of Neptune. A sketch by

Francisco d'Hoĺlanda shows the fountain in its former splendor. At the far end of this garden is a pedimented door flanked by two crumbling stucco giants, who once had weapons on their shoulders. These were made by Baccio Bandinelli and guard the entrance to the woods beyond. The path through the woods ended in a semicircle. Below the Piazzale della Fontana is a sustaining wall with niches and fountain jets emptying into a rectangular fishpond. This lower terrace was an orange garden and is reached by walled stairways. At the northern corner of this terrace is the third tower leading to a long terrace originally planned to run the length of the villa.

The garden was designed to be viewed as a whole from the base of Monte Mario. It was planned to ascend the hillside by an allée beginning from the stables located at Ponte Molle, climb up to the villa, pass through a smaller loggia to the circular courtyard, and continue into a stepped amphitheater built against the hillside. By further steps and ramps one could climb to the summit of the wooded hill. This much is attributed to Raphael, as well as a plan of three garden spaces, linked with long flights of steps following their contours. However, several drawings in the Uffizi of these linked gardens are attributed to the Sangallo family. To begin with, there is a square with four-part beds and a central square fountain, which is adjacent to the second space; a circular enclosure has three niches and long curving steps; the third compartment is a large hemicycle planned as a horse track. One can only speculate where this triple garden was to have been constructed in relationship to the villa itself, a debate that began when Percier and Fontaine published their *Maisons de Plaisance de Rome* in 1809, followed up by Geymuller, Coffin, and Dami. No documents exist other than the two Uffizi plans attributed to Francesco da Sangallo to prove the proposed garden's relation to the rest of the property. However, a clue lies in the indication of the circular stairway connected to the square garden. It is believed that this circular stair is one of the corner towers. From the topography of the hill, this proposed garden series proba-

Villa Madama, watercolor by J. C. Shepherd (1925). British Architectural Library, R.I.B.A., London.

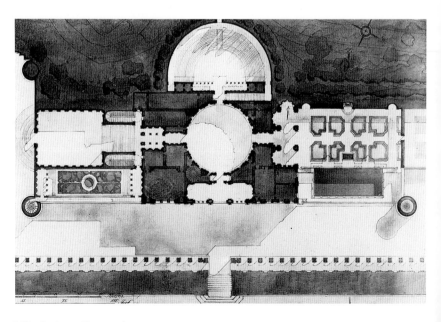

bly lay on the southeastern end of the property. To connect it on a north-south axis would overlap another proposed squared garden, adjacent to the allée; but, more important, the hippodrome would have covered a very uneven terrain. In the southeastern location it would also be nearer to the stables and allée for access.

Nestled in a small valley northwest of the villa was to have been another linked garden. This would have been entered at the end of a walk from the Piazzale della Fontana straight through the *bosco*. According to the Uffizi drawing attributed to Francesco da Sangallo, the first garden was to have had four compartments plus a half-circle with fountain at the northern end. Adjacent to the west was a garden ending in a *nymphaeum*, not well defined, which would have had a fountain. This probably is the garden referred to in payments for the garden of "vignia del papa" in 1524 and 1525 during the papacy of Clement. The summary sketches are labeled "Fontana della valle."

Villa Borghese

The gardens of Villa Borghese seem fragmented because the present park comprises various parcels of land, hundreds of acres loosely linked together, incorporating gardens of different eras. Over the years the plan has been redesigned to better unite the disparate elements as well as to cater to the changing fashions in garden taste. (Of the original seventeenth-century garden, a few architectural details remain around the villa.)

A visitor is apt to see portions of the garden on successive visits: a trip to the famed Museo Borghese in the villa brings one to the core of the original garden, imperfectly preserved, but skips the rest of the garden approached from the Pincian hill, or traversed in a taxi en route to Via Veneto. The Romans since the seventeenth century have claimed the garden as their own and make full use of it.

Early in the seventeenth century, Don Scipione Caffarelli possessed vineyards formerly belonging to the dukes d'Altemps in the Pincian zone. In 1605 his uncle, Paul V, made him a cardinal. He took the pope's family name of Borghese together with the family dragon crest. Cardinal Borghese purchased ten additional vineyards and parcels. He hired Giovanni Vasanzio (Il Fiammingo) to build the villa between 1605 and 1613. The villa has two square towers, and jutting foreblocks connected by a balconied loggia and double ramp entrance staircase. Following the example of neighboring Villa Medici, the outer surface was encrusted with antique bas-reliefs and busts, later plucked out by Napoleon for his collection at the Louvre.

The original gardens that clustered around the villa were designed by Girolamo Rainaldi. Domenico Savino later expanded the gardens, and Giovanni Fontana designed the waterworks. Pietro Bernini did some sculpture and fountains (including the two puffy genial herms now in the Metropolitan Museum of Art, New York). From Giovanni Falda's print we can reconstruct the early state of the garden. The villa's rectangular forecourt is still bordered by the elaborate balustrade ornamented by the Borghese dragons, its entrance marked by spitting fountain masks over lobed basins, surmounted by a pair of Roman statues. A viale connects the villa to the Porta Pinciana. The twenty-eight hedged squares are filled with trees and form intersections for the viales facing the villa. Some form exedras and are decorated with antique sarcophagi, statues, and columns. Ponzio in 1609 created the large exedra within the garden at Porta Pinciana. Holm oak, cypresses, and stone pines cluster in the area around the villa. Flanking the villa were two long, walled flower gardens. At the end of the western one is a fantastic aviary with double domes and ten portrait busts in

niches, the creation of Luigi Vanvitelli between 1617 and 1619. This was inspired by the aviary of the Orti Farnesiani. John Evelyn refers to it in his description of the garden (*Diary*, ed. E. S. de Beer, 1959):

> The garden abounded with all sorts of delicious fruits and exotic simples, fountains of sundry inventions, groves, and small rivulets. There is also adjoining to it a vivarium for ostriches, peacocks, swans, cranes, etc., and divers strange beasts, deer and hares. The grotto is very rare, and represents, among other devices artificial rain. . . . The four sphinxes are very ancient. To this is a volary full of curious birds.

Behind the villa is a semi-oval courtyard with a simple box parterre garden, bordered by antique statues, large caryatid figures balancing fruit on their heads, and enormous globes on pedestals. The fountain originally had a bronze statue of Narcissus, now replaced by Venus. In the northwest corner of the woods, which in earlier times stood behind the courtyard, an exedra forming an open-air theater was built between 1613 and 1616. The villa was rebuilt and a new garden plan designed when Prince Marcantonio IV inherited the property in 1763. The plan of Falda appears little changed in Percier and Fontaine's plan of 1809, but radical changes were effected by the landscape designers Jacob Moore and Pietro Camporesi.

Villa Borghese, from Triggs, *Art of Garden Design . . .* (1906).

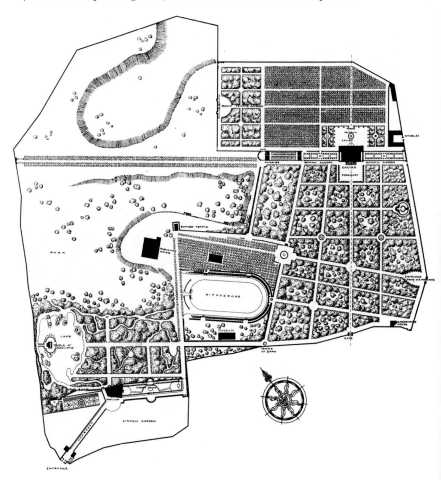

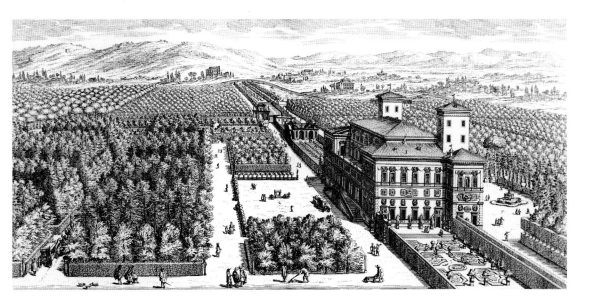

View of Villa Borghese and its park, from G. B. Falda, *Ville e giardini di Roma* (1683).

The hippodrome, known as the Piazza di Siena, was built in a gentle valley in 1792. Two rows of magnificent stone pines shade the grassy spectator steps overlooking the 650-foot-long course.

At the furthermost point southwest, Moore designed a true English landscape garden with shady wandering paths and a free-form artificial lake. On a small island, the eighteenth-century Ionic temple houses a large statue of Aesculapius, the Greek hero and god of healing who was imported to Rome to ward off a plague in the second century B.C. From the edges of the woody island, river gods pour water into the lake, which is populated by ducks and row boats. This area—comprising a well-tended, formal parterre, views over the city, and a restaurant—is much frequented.

There remain the vast open rolling fields studded with plane trees, originally the deer park or hunting preserve, which now contains the city zoo.

Napoleon's sister Pauline married Don Camillo Borghese. The two were ill-suited; Pauline's frivolity and lavish life-style drove Don Camillo away to Florence. (A reclining nude statue of Pauline by Antonio Canova is one of the treasures of the villa's collection.) Napoleon forced Don Camillo to sell his large collection of antiquities to France. He was a Republican at heart, burning the papal arms and dancing in the streets at the liberty festivities, which led to his formal exile from Rome during the Restoration. In 1820 he purchased adjoining properties, expanding the total circumference to over four miles with five entrances. Luigi Canina was given the task of connecting the new and old portions of the garden. He built a drive from the Piazzale Flaminio to the lake. The piazzale was marked by an Egyptian-style pylon gate. Two new viales decorated with obelisks and colonnades linked the lake garden to the villa. A triumphal arch faced the lake garden. The nineteenth-century additions were eclectic, inspired by the craze for the Neoclassical and recent excavations in Egypt and at Hadrian's villa outside Rome.

Prince Marcantonio Borghese decided to divide up and develop the

property in 1885. The mayor, Leopoldo Torlonia, blocked this, basing his case on a plaque installed on a wall of the villa in 1620, which invited the public to enjoy the park freely, stating that its creation was more for the benefit of the public than that of the proprietor. In fact the lake garden, added between 1786 and 1787, was designed to be a private walled-off retreat for the Borghese family, while the remaining park was open to the public.

The former Casino of Graziano in the large valley of plane trees now serves as the entrance to the zoo. Among the other pavilions in the park were a fake ruined fortress, a chapel, and a temple to Diana with a bronze, tiled dome and delicate masks. The Pavilion of the Orologio, or water-clock, still functioning, was completed in 1688.

The various gates are worthy of note. Originally there were two principal ones: at Porta del Popolo and Porta Pinciano, with a third smaller one on an axis to the villa.

The state purchased the property from the Borghese family in 1902 for three million lire. Despite an attempt to change the name to Villa Umberto Primo, it remains known as the "Villa Borghese."

Closing one's eyes to the asphalt viales and traffic it is possible to imagine it as it must have been centuries ago.

Villa Medici

Rome
Gardens open to the public
on Wednesday mornings

Villa Medici, from G. Vasi, *Magnificenze di Roma* (1747–59).

Built on the Pincio, Villa Medici dominates Rome. Commissioned by one cardinal and completed by another, the villa now houses the Académie de France. Villa Medici's importance as a garden is twofold—first, as the best preserved of the Roman Renaissance garden plans, second, for its links to the fine arts—for it is the site of a great collection of antiquities and a source of inspiration for over three hundred years of creative work by French artists.

The garden design is not complex; it is built against a hillside with several levels and gentle slopes. The lines are straight, marking off squared sections by rows of cypresses and high clipped box hedges. A grove of ilex opens onto a round, open area. Palms and magnolias soften the effect around the villa's piazzale and flower beds. Its famed far-reaching views over the city become an extension of the garden itself; the garden was planned with this in mind, with a mount topped by a belvedere, terraces at various locations, and openings in the circuit wall for no other purpose

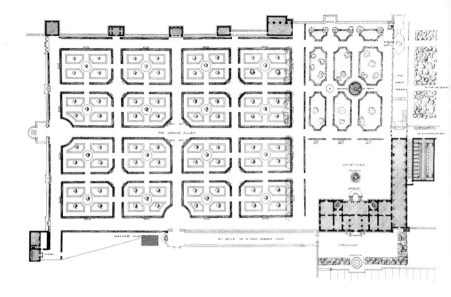

than to provide views of the world beyond the garden. At sunset the city below takes on a violet hue, all seven hills are visible, and the major monuments can be made out, the dome of Saint Peter's rises high over the city.

The Pincian hill was anciently planted with the gardens of Lucullus, Sallust, and Domitian and known as the *collis horticulorum.* Today the gardens of Villa Borghese and the Pincio border those of Villa Medici, creating a vast green area on the map of Rome.

The cream-colored villa with twin square towers faces the city as if it were a fortress; the lower portion has substantial bastions. In the late seventeenth century Queen Christina of Sweden "knocked" on the villa's door by firing shots from Castel Sant'Angelo across the river in order to summon the owner of Villa Medici to a hunt. The portal still displays the scars.

The modest villa bought by Cardinal Crescenzi in 1540 was enlarged by the architect Nanni di Banco Bigi. The gardens were simple, consisting primarily of vineyards. His heirs sold the property to Cardinal Giovanni Ricci di Montepulciano who hired Nanni's son, Annibale Lippi, to continue the project and redesign the garden facade. Great sums were spent over a decade embellishing the villa and its gardens with orchards and a supply of water.

After Cardinal Ricci's death, it was sold to Ferdinando de'Medici in 1576. By 1581 it was considered the most lavish villa in Rome. Ferdinando de'Medici was made a cardinal at the tender age of fifteen. His amiable, generous, and disinterested disposition endeared him to the Romans. He was the *éminence grise* to the lackadaisical pope Gregory XIII and curbed Sixtus V. Patron of the sculptor Giambologna, and collector of antiquities on a vast scale, he adorned the villa richly. The villa was in its heyday during his stay. He planted the ilex, myrtle, and added fountains. However, his brother, the grand duke of Tuscany, died without male heir, and Ferdinando was recalled to Florence to take his place, setting aside his church vows. After his departure in 1587, much of the choice statuary gradually followed him to Florence. The group of Niobe and her Fourteen Children, mentioned in Pliny's account, had been in the garden under a special enclosure against the west wall. Removed to Florence in 1775 they are now in the Uffizi. The famous Medici vase and Giambologna's Mercury vanished from the villa's loggia. The two monumental lions that guarded the loggia were moved to Florence's Piazza della Signoria under the Loggia de'Lanzi. During Jean-August Ingres's tenure as director of the Académie in Rome (1834–41) he ordered copies made of the missing principal statues, and these grace the loggia today.

Following Ferdinando, Alessandro de'Medici of Naples (later the short-lived pope Leo XI) added a fountain before the garden facade. While pope in 1605 he banned the beautiful Venus de'Medici as indecent, sending her away to Florence where she is now the centerpiece of the Tribuna in the Uffizi. During this period, Marie de'Medici lived in the villa until her marriage to King Henri IV of France.

The Villa Medici provided a haven for Galileo from persecution by the Inquisition between 1633 and 1634. He named the satellites of Jupiter the "Stars of the Medici" after his patrons.

Dated 4 December 1787, an inventory of Grand Duke Ferdinando II of Lorraine detailed the statuary, fruit trees, fountains, and vines. At that time the five hundred fruit trees included pears, peaches, pineapples, apples, quinces, figs, mulberries, almonds, and oranges. In 1801 the heirs of the Medici sold the villa to the duke of Parma, who two years later exchanged it with the French Republic for the Palazzo Salviati.

Throughout the peaceful gardens are scattered studios occupied by the recipients, or "pensioners" of the four-year Grand Prix de Rome. They have housed the painters Boucher, Ingres, Fragonard, David, Hubert-Robert, and Balthus; the sculptors Coustou, Pagalle, Rude, Carpeaux, and Houdin, as well as musicians including Debussy, Berlioz, Gounod, and Bizet. The Académie de France was the brainchild of French minister Jean-Baptiste Colbert to produce court art for Louis XIV and founded in 1666. The Grand Prix de Rome was instituted in 1767. When the pensioners were here in the nineteenth century they were expected to make copies, drawings, and plans of all the masterpieces in Rome.

The garden's lines are severe, yet restful. The shady approach drive leads to a small belvedere terrace to the left and the straight allées dividing the high box hedges into square compartments. Tucked into carved niches in the green walls are bits and pieces of sarcophagi, oil jars, and busts. Behind the villa, the garden opens up.

The soaring Mercury looks across an axis defined by two round fountains, the obelisk, and low-hedged parterre sections, ending in the colossal statue of the goddess Roma. To the east of the parterre is a niched wall, possibly originally a lemon house, sustaining a terrace above. This wall is separated from the villa's gallery by the long central axis, which leads to the gate at Via Pinciana. The eastern portion of the garden consists of a *boschetto*, a mount, a lemon garden, and a small flower garden behind the gallery. The existence of a mount is a curiosity in Italy, more typical of English gardens, or gardens planted on flat terrain. This mount, or "mausoleum," has a spiral path with sixty steps lined with cypresses, terminating in a circular loggia known as the Temple of the Sun. Gabriele D'Annunzio used the setting at sunset for his romantic novel *Il Piacere*.

Il Quirinale

Rome
Gardens open upon request:
Palazzo del Quirinale
Palace Administration
Via della Dataria
Rome

The Quirinale's gardens were first laid out for Cardinal Ippolito d'Este, the same man who created the famed   Este gardens of Tivoli. This was to be his Roman summer palazzo set on Monte Cavallo, the highest of the Roman hills at two hundred feet, site of the ancient Temple of the Sun. This spot was appreciated by popes for its pure healthy air from the time of Gregory XIII (1572–85) until 1870. Despite the health-giving air, twenty-two of the twenty-nine presiding popes died here.

The garden is composed of bay, box, and palms, with the occasional huge ilex tree, survivors of those planted four hundred years ago by Cardinal Ippolito. The garden is long and stretches the entire width of the property, undercut through the middle by the tunnel of Traforo Umberto I. Bordering both sides of the length of the garden are enormous clipped

Il Quirinale, from G. B. Falda, *Ville e giardini di Roma* (1683).

hedges of bay and box, wide enough for roads to be cut through and over thirty feet in height. An old layout seen in Antonio Nolli's print of 1748 consists of fifty-nine prim square parterres; remaining only in part today, the low hedges have mushroomed and grown tall, obscuring the overall view and creating long, shady, mysterious allées with openings into garden rooms with fountains. These dense paths, with their perspectives reaching to the far ends of the garden, the silence in the heart of Rome, and the groves of spectacular palm trees, give the garden its character today. Scattered throughout are bits and pieces of ancient Roman and Renaissance urns, sarcophagi, and statuary. A particularly handsome freestanding stone sundial stands within the palm garden to the west. Near the palazzo is Ferdinando Fuga's graceful eighteenth-century pavilion. Facing it is a round pool with water nymphs perched on a rock in the center. These statues were brought from the royal gardens of Caserta. The terrain drops steeply beneath a terrace garden planted with parterres and rose hedges. A splendid view of Monte Mario and Saint Peter's is enjoyed from here. Peering over the balcony one can see the crumbling remains of the great Organ Fountain in its courtyard below the palazzo.

The gardens date back to the mid-sixteenth century when Cardinal Ippolito d'Este first rented the land from the Carafas. To this, Pius IV added a vineyard, which the church had confiscated from Leonardo Boccacci. The early garden consisted of a parterre by Ottavio Mascherino, grottoes, and fountains. Among the works designed by Girolamo da Carpi for this garden were wooden temple-like enclosures for the statuary. Carlo Maderno, architect of San Andrea della Valle, designed the early waterworks. Possibly Pirro Ligorio designed ramps on the steep slope. He was chief architect of Este's garden at Tivoli and directed works for two gardens on Monte Cavallo. The botanist, Evangelista Quattrami, long connected with the Este family, added rare plants.

Gregory XIII takes credit for the building of the Quirinale Palazzo, and by 1584 he was residing there. It was his habit to stroll through the gardens in the middle of the night. A grotto fountain with his coat-of-arms was his contribution to the gardens. His successor Sixtus V continued and expanded the palace construction.

The Aldobrandini pope, Clement VIII, had Giovanni Fontana design the monumental Organ Fountain, or "Nicchione," between 1595 and 1597, set below the palazzo in an open-air hall. Pompeo Maderno did the hydraulics and Giovanni Giacomo Neri the mosaic works. Flanking the organ were the Halls of Cyclops and Vulcan.

In 1597 Jean-Jacques Boissard praised the extraordinary ingenuity of the garden's features, the variety of its trees, the interlacing branches above a labyrinth, and the fact that all the walls were covered as if carpeted by citrus, pomegranates, and odiferous herbs, providing year-round pleasure unsurpassed by any other Roman garden.

A more encompassing, tighter garden plan was laid out after the garden was extended towards the Via delle Quattro Fontane. This can be studied in the engraving of a bird's-eye view of the garden done in 1612 by Giovanni Maggi. Much of the conception of the new plan was due to Paul V, himself. He acquired additional lands from the monks of Messina to set off the Quirinale and its gardens. The central portion of the garden was redesigned with straight paths and parterres centered around a fountain. At

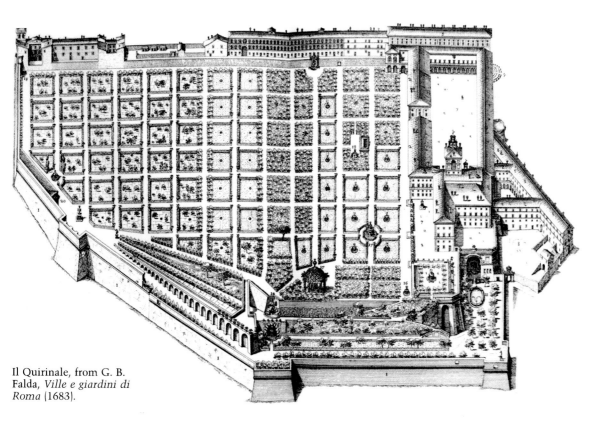

Il Quirinale, from G. B. Falda, *Ville e giardini di Roma* (1683).

that time the principal fountain was that of the "Umbrella." On the right a grove surrounded a tower and rustic fountain. On the left the ground sloped down and the plantings were informal. The so-called Temple was a domed, round building with four cupolas. The Fountain of Porphyry was set under a trellised, leafy canopy. A secret parterre garden was set upon a raised terrace by the end of the palace. Other fountains included "the mirror," "the dog statue," "the little bridges," and a duplex fountain of "the flood and the rain." Giovanni Falda's slightly later view shows a central enormous parterre plan; gone is the large informal grove to the far side. Disciplined rows of trees have been planted traversing and bordering the gardens, but the effect is monotonous.

In 1625 Urban VIII enclosed the Quirinale grounds with fortresslike walls, adding still more fountains. Benedict XIV commissioned Ferdinando Fuga to build a caffehaus in 1741 and rearranged the area around it. Pompeo Batoni, Cocciolini, Carl Bloeman, and Francesco Pannini decorated the pavilion. Pannini painted the meeting of King Carlo III of Naples and the pope at the elegant caffehaus. Indeed, Benedict so preferred the Quirinale to the Vatican that most of his reign was spent here.

Restorations of the caffehaus and organ were effected under Gregory XVI (1831–46), who also added a labyrinth of box and erected a Swiss chalet. He cut a long, central allée through the grand parterre area, lining the path with large lemon pots and palm trees, marking it with a fountain by Martucci. The design of the garden today is much as he left it.

Napoleon's troops marched into the Quirinale and seized Pius VII on 7 July 1809, carrying him off to Fontainebleau. Again in 1870 the doors were forced, and the Quirinale was lost to the Papacy. From that time on it has been the property of the Italian State. It served as a residence of the Italian monarchy, and now houses the president of the Republic.

Orti Farnesiani

Rome
Gardens open to the public

Few are aware when scaling the hill linking the Forum to the Palatine that they are treading on what was the famed sixteenth-century Orti Farnesiani, one of the major botanical gardens of the Renaissance. Initially, the designer was the master garden architect Giacomo Barozzi da Vignola, who worked for Pope Paul III. During his reign (1534–49), the pope began construction of the Orti over the ruins of the palaces of the emperors Tiberius and Domitian. His nephews, Cardinals Alessandro and Ottaviano, carried out the plans after his death. Paul III was a knowledgeable botanist who revitalized the Vatican gardens, but his enthusiasm was focused primarily on the Orti Farnesiani, which were renowned in their day for their rare plants, listed by Tobia Aldini in 1625 in *Exactissima descriptio rariorum quarundam plantarum, quae continentur Romae in Horto Farnesiano.* Many specimens were imported from the Americas, including the *Agave americana,* the Passion Flower of Peru, and the "Farnesian" acacia from the island of San Domingo.

There is some question as to the extent of Vignola's hand in the overall design. I suspect that Vignola designed the portion covering the slope: the triple-terraced slope with its ramps and stairways forming promenades to the hilltop, 160 feet above the Forum. It has the breadth of design and decisive perspective axis associated with the architect. Chronologically the Orti Farnesiani precede his Villa Giulia and Villa Farnese at Caprarola. Certainly he designed the great entrance portal that stood in Campo Vaccino. Some suggest that the portal's upper portion was by Giacomo del Duca, a slavish follower of Michelangelo, and hence the suggestion of Michelangelo's participation in the garden. Others attribute the entire garden design to Girolamo Rainaldi. Since Rainaldi was not born until 1570 this seems unlikely despite the long delay in construction as evidenced by a map from 1577 and a painted view of Rome, from about 1588, showing only the completed portal, the hillside remaining unlandscaped (although this could be an artistic simplification). After Vignola's death in 1573, his work at Caprarola was carried out by Giacomo del Duca and considerably later by Rainaldi, both of whom worked at the Orti Farnesiani. It is probable that they followed Vignola's pre-existing designs for the Orti, embellishing the aviary-water theater with Rainaldi's fountain, and designing the upper level themselves.

Formerly set in a high wall, pierced by windows overlooking the Forum, the arched portal has a rusticated lower portion; above this a second arch is crowned by a broken pediment. On the ground level terrace was a

Gli Orti Farnesiani, from G. Vasi, *Magnificenze di Roma* (1747–59).

semicircular enclosure, bisected by a ramp leading to a pilastered portico. Behind it was the Room of the Rain, which received water from the fountain on the terrace above it. The Fountain of the Rain was built in 1612 by Rainaldi. The room was lined with eight statues and twelve busts, many brought from Hadrian's villa. Ramps wound up around the fountain to the second and third promenade terraces. Here on an axis with the entrance portal was the water theater flanked by double staircases with twin domed aviaries (which later would inspire those at Villa Borghese). Kneeling before them were two large statues of moors holding up vases. The hillside below was planted with rows of trees; a long narrow parterre cut by a ramp filled the space between the second and third terraces. The fourth level was the plateau of the Monte Palatino. It was divided up into squares, traversed by a central viale from the aviary, to a vantage point over the Circus Maximus. There were four transverse viales. The box-enclosed squares varied in content and size. To the west was a belvedere overlooking the Forum. At the far end, the garden dissolved into excavations. Other features included a fountain surrounded by plane trees near the aviary, and two rectangular fishponds facing a mosaic grotto containing the Fountain of Mirrors, reached by two descending flights of steps (traces of this still exist). There was a small casino overlooking a walled secret garden in the far corner of the garden.

Here between 1693 and 1699 the Academy of Arcadians met before they were transferred to the Bosco Parrasio (another fascinating, but tiny private garden, well conserved).

The Orti Farnesiani descended to the Bourbons of Naples through Elisabetta Farnese. The gardens suffered much neglect over the years. In 1822

186 · *Latium, Campania*

the upper gardens were mostly destroyed to facilitate excavations. A mask
and basin from the original gardens have been moved to Piazza Santa Sabi-
na. The majestic effect of Vignola's hillside has been lost, overgrown now,
and his portal transported to nearby Via Gregorio. The upper level today
has been replanted as a flower garden and public park, without regard for
the original design.

Vatican Gardens

Rome
*Gardens open to the public
through conducted tours
in the morning (apply at
the Ufficio Pellegrini,
Piazza San Pietro)*

The Vatican gardens have always been used by the popes for their private moments, a much needed breath of fresh air from the musty, confining halls of the Vatican. They have meditated and exercised in the gardens, remained in retreat in the casino, or recently, in the Saracen tower, and held informal gatherings in the Villa Pia's courtyard. Indeed, some popes, including Pius IV in the sixteenth century, have spent every possible hour here, dictating letters in the summer house, meeting with their cardinals in the Belvedere courtyard, and returning to the interior of the Vatican only for vespers. It is not surprising therefore, that the individual popes have placed their mark upon the gardens, incorporating their family emblems into commissioned works.

The papal gardens sprawl up a hillside to the rear of the basilica and the Vatican palace. There is no unifying garden design. Areas of varying periods are loosely linked together by a carriage drive laid out in the latter half of the nineteenth century. Consulting maps and engravings of the gardens over the centuries, one is struck by the constant alterations, eliminations, and expansions. Although the Vatican city was completely enclosed by walls in 852, the first attempt to tame the hillside was made only in the late thirteenth century under Nicholas III, who planted extensive orchards. A true garden plan was drawn up by Leon Battista Alberti in 1450

Garden of Villa Pia, The Vatican, from G. B. Falda, *Le Fontane di Roma* (1675–91).

for Nicholas V; unfortunately we can only guess at its design. We know that the vineyard included a fishpond and fountain, and that there was a *giardino segreto*. Pius I embellished this latter element with a wooden pavilion and pergola between 1461 and 1463, and in 1470 Paul II added an eight pillared fountain. There is no trace of this garden today. Innocent VIII built the Villa Belvedere between 1484 and 1492, planting a simple garden surrounding it.

The tri-partite courtyard design of the Belvedere with its terraced stairways was of immense importance to Roman garden design as it was the first to unite villa and garden. The fifteenth-century Villa of the Belvedere was separated from the papal palace by a valley. Julius II had Donato Bramante design a linking courtyard, which was begun in 1503. Bramante envisioned leveling a portion of the valley and connecting the existing buildings by two long two-story wings topped by colonnades to the lawn level of the Belvedere. There, a third shorter wing with a large central niche would be the focus of the courtyard. Within there were to be three levels of terraces connected with broad wide steps; a sustaining wall on the second level was composed of three niches set off with columns. During Bramante's tenure only the right-hand wing and the third short wing were partially completed. Many years would pass before the other long wing was built. It is not known with certainty what Bramante's ideas were for the plantings. Raphael designed early parterres for this courtyard, and went on to work on the gardens of Villa Madama, borrowing the structural ideas of terraced stairways. The Belvedere became a display site for such treasures as the Apollo Belvedere and Laocoön.

What is seen today is a truncated courtyard, unhappily divided in two by the wing of the Biblioteca and Braccio Nuovo. The courtyard was near completion during the pontificate of Sixtus V (1585–90), lacking only some steps and details. Sixtus V hired Domenico Fontana to build the library, thus destroying the effect of Bramante's progressive terraces and the perspective culminating in the niche.

For many years orchards were located just beyond the Belvedere courtyard. Early in the sixteenth century, Paul III enclosed them as one walled garden with a medieval style crisscross vaulted *berceaux* marking the paths, giving place later to flower beds edged with trees. This area is now a lemon garden.

The most enchanting part of the garden is found halfway down the slope towards the Vatican museum, hidden from above by a thick grove of umbrella pines. This is Pirro Ligorio's casino, the Villa Pia, which was the first Italian garden house to be built in seclusion, as a retreat, setting the fashion for all others that followed, starting with the casino at Caprarola. It was begun in 1560 for Pius IV, whose name it bears. Adapted from ancient Roman models carefully studied by Ligorio, Villa Pia consists of two pavilions linked by an oval courtyard with two gateways. The upper pavilion has three stories containing several rooms. The pavilion opposite is basically an open loggia. The facades are decorated with stucco bas-reliefs and colored mosaics, some of the material undoubtedly transported from the emperor Domitian's circus in Piazza Navona. The courtyard's marble-patterned floor sets off the central fountain with putti riding dolphins. Water from it flows beneath the loggia to a large basin presided over by the sea nymph Thetis enthroned in a niche. The exterior wall here is bright with mosaics reflected in the waters, an effect Ligorio borrowed from the ancient Romans. The gregarious and witty Pius IV met here with the intellects of his court, including his nephew and close advisor, San Carlo Borromeo, for informal recitations of poetry and philosophical discussions. With the Reformation, these secular discourses were banned. Leo X included ladies in gatherings held here for banquets, concerts, and poetry readings. The casino now houses the Academy of Science. As seen in Giovanni Falda's print, there were parterre beds radiating in star-shaped fashion from this casino—a model for future French gardens. These were unfortunately

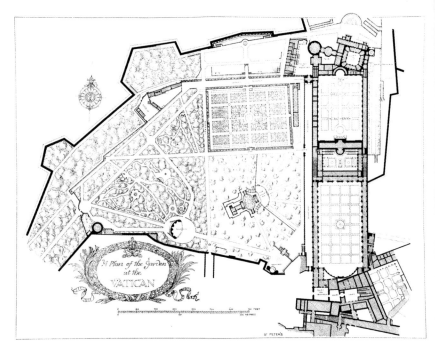

destroyed when Pius V allowed his physician to live in the casino; the
doctor replanted the beds randomly with medicinal herbs and exotics. In
the nineteenth century, under Gregory XVI, the beds were totally torn up
and the area refashioned with lawns and trees planted *à l'anglaise.* Nearby,
groves of ilex and birch contain antiquities scattered under their branches,
pagan reminders that these slopes were originally the site of the gardens of
Agrippina and Domitian in the first century, and temples to Nero, Apollo,
and Mars stood here before the basilica was built. As if to counter the pagan past, Michelangelo's dome is visible from most areas of the garden.

At the end of one long remaining ninth-century wall within the garden is the Saracen's tower. It was defended by volunteer soldiers against
the French. Earlier this century John XXIII had the tower restored and
lived in it while the Vatican palace was being renovated. John Paul II
chose to live here for three months in 1981.

In 1929, with the Conciliation of Church and State ending the Vatican
"Captivity"—a political conflict between the Italian government and the
Church's temporal authority during which time the pope remained "cap-
tive" in the Vatican—numerous structures were built within the garden,
such as the large Palazzo of the Propagation of the Faith, Guglielmo
Marconi's radio station, a train station, and so forth. As a result, a large
formal garden was swept away, no great loss as its fussy scale
lacked an overall coherence. Further up the hill, a sunken rectangular parterre of clipped greens and white gravel with two round fountains was installed. Placed near it is a rose garden in the Vatican colors of yellow and
white, with jasmine arches and fountains. The large Grotto to Our Lady of
Lourdes is found beyond it. The garden additionally contains a hothouse
for succulents, and a proper vegetable garden for the pope's own table. One
rocky slope is planted with alpine flowers, a rarity in Italy.

Villa Doria Pamphili

Rome
Gardens open to the public

To the southwest of the Janiculan hills sprawl the vast gardens of the Villa Doria Pamphili, formerly known as Villa Belrespiro for the superior quality of its air and remarkably mild climate.

The seventeenth-century gardens were built on the supposed site of ancient gardens belonging to the emperor Galba, who was believed to have been murdered by his Praetorians, then buried here by his faithful slave Argius. Subsequently it became a luxurious cemetery with streets and houselike tombs. As a result, when the villa was built around 1650 on top of this site, a wealth of antique sculptures surfaced in the excavations. Many fragments were used to ornament the villa's facade after the style of Villa Medici. Other pieces found a new setting in the gardens; moss-covered sarcophagi and statues are scattered in the extensive pine forest.

Panfilio Pamphili made the first acquisition of land here in 1630. This consisted of the purchase of a vineyard and rustic village from Giacomo Rotolo. Over the years until the nineteenth century, the property was greatly expanded with forty-six additional purchased pieces, totaling 520 acres and running a perimeter of five and one-half miles, part of it bordered by the old Via Aurelia. (Today the area has been substantially trimmed down; much of the hunting preserve sacrificed to new housing, and the construction of the Via Olympica through the property.)

Credit for the creation of the villa belongs to Donna Olympia Maidal-

Fountain of the Water Theater at Villa Doria Pamphili, from G. B. Falda, *Le Fontane di Roma* (1675–91).

Villa Doria Pamphili, engraving by G. B. Piranesi (18th century).

chini. Twice widowed, with three sons, she seized upon the rising star of her brother-in-law, Cardinal Giambattista Pamphili. In 1644 when he became Pope Innocent X, she dominated the papacy, insisting on special personal privileges, such as a seat under a baldachino and a canopied litter for her frequent transport to the Vatican. She had access to all the most powerful men of the day, including entry to the monasteries—normally off limits to women. Favors were dispensed through her influence; no decisions were taken by the pope without consulting Olympia. She greedily amassed an enormous fortune, enriching her sons as well in the process. This villa was built by her for one of them—Camillo Pamphili, who renounced an ecclesiastical career for marriage. Olympia's portrait bust by Alessandro Algardi depicts a haughty, self-indulgent personality.

When a pope was elected it was customary for the mob to sack the pope's family palace. Anticipating this, Olympia prudently emptied the palace of valuables. Not unnaturally the Roman populace was enraged by her conduct and wrote pointed satires *(pasquinades)* about "Olympia Impia" (Olympia the Impious). As the pope became feeble in his final illness, Olympia moved him out of the Vatican into her Trastevere villa, and guarded him day and night. According to legend, a fiery horseman rode through the gardens of Villa Doria Pamphili in premonition of the death of Innocent X. At the end, Olympia was banned from the death chamber, but returned to retrieve boxes of gold from under the pope's bed. She tried to bribe the new pope, Alexander VII, but was roundly rebuffed and strongly advised to leave Rome.

Olympia and Camillo Pamphili planned a casino for papal entertaining, to hold banquets and receptions. At first Francesco Borromini was consulted. He drew up a plan that was influenced by the fortress-like villa of Caprarola. Rejected, the drawings survive today in the Biblioteca Apostolica Vaticana (Codice Vaticano Latino). The project passed to the sculptor Alessandro Algardi, who, together with a landscape painter, Giovan Francesco Grimaldi, created the existing villa shortly after 1644.

The gardens of the Villa Doria Pamphili consist basically of three sections: the formal gardens immediately around the house, including the entrance drive and the parterred sunken garden behind the villa; a larger central lower area with an amphitheater, its plantings transformed over the years; and finally a vast park planted with pines and ilex avenues, with a canal carrying water to a lake set in a natural hunting preserve. The early layout had precise avenues with axial perspective views, in great part destroyed in the nineteenth century by the unfortunate replanting à l'anglaise.

The secret garden has most closely preserved its original aspect. It is backed by the villa and closed by walls at either end, a handsome balustrade topped with potted orange trees looks south. The garden is planted with *broderie* box parterres between fishponds with simple bronze fleur-de-lis fountains. In the center is a copy of Pietro Tacca's Demon Fountain from Piazza Santissima Annunziata in Florence, added in the nineteenth century. This garden is particularly protected from winds by its southern exposure. A double staircase meets below the Fountain of Venus and sweeps down to ground level. As seen in Piranesi's print of the eighteenth century, this ground level originally had high hedges enclosing lemon trees, similar to those at the entrance of the villa. The large semicircular amphitheater, rimmed with ilex and ornamented with niches, pilasters, and statuary has survived. Ramps lead to the upper terrace; beneath the structure is a *salle fraiche* (a cool garden retreat built into a hillside), similar to that of Frascati's Villa Aldobrandini. A passageway cuts through the hill behind, emerging in a grotto. To the right of the amphitheater are the remains of a rusticated water theater with niches and a pool in front. This had a *nymphaeum* with a faun playing a bagpipe in the center niche; its wings had eighteen smaller fountains; sirens played in the pool.

Villa Doria Pamphili, from Triggs, *Art of Garden Design . . .* (1906).

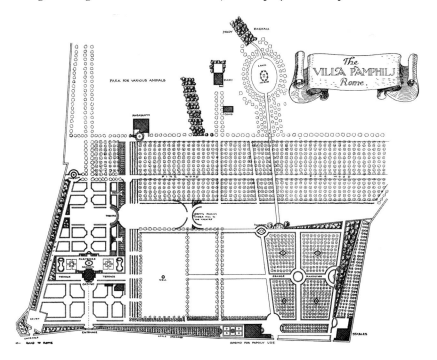

After the death of the last male Pamphili, the grand-niece of Pope Innocent X became the sole descendant of the family. She married Andrea III Doria Landi in 1671, and the property thus passed to the Doria family. In 1783, some changes were made to the garden under the architect Giovanni Antinori for Andrea Doria. In the first half of the nineteenth century, Filippo Andrea V Doria Pamphili married Lady Mary Talbot, who was responsible for the modernizing of large portions of the garden, and marking it with a stand of large cut cypresses spelling out "MARY." She destroyed the formal planting around the amphitheater. Instead, amid lawns and palm trees, is the large Fountain of Cupid and the Angels, designed by Paolo Ameli and Francesco Niccoletti, who in this period designed various fountains and gates for the garden. Lady Mary also placed the copy of the Tacca fountain in the secret garden.

Le Nôtre came to Rome in 1678, about thirty years after the villa was built. According to tradition, Le Nôtre designed these gardens, but earlier plans depict the layout much as it remained in Antonio Nolli's map of 1748. Perhaps Le Nôtre suggested the *broderie* patterns or the rows of pines, but it is highly unlikely. He was in Rome to study the Italian garden style, not to create his own designs.

In its day the garden was famed for its magnificent view from the entrance terrace, encompassing the Roman countryside and the dome of Saint Peter's. It was also noted for its variety of fountains described by G. P. Bellori in his *Vite dei pittori, scultori, architetti moderni* (1672). Among these was the Fountain of the Snail near the villa. This was a delightful fountain designed by Bernini for Piazza Navona, but turned down due to its insignificant scale. Pope Innocent then presented it to his sister-in-law, who placed it here. The original has since been removed to the Doria Pamphili Landi apartments, and a nineteenth-century copy is in its place.

The Fountain of the Regina was a focal point of a perspective allée. It still exists with slender, wide arched jets of water issuing from the dolphin atop a tiered basin. The Fountain of the Dolphins, set in the pine woods, was destroyed in the nineteenth century in order to use the site for a neo-Romanesque chapel by Odoardo Collamarini. The eighteenth century saw the addition of the Fountain of Venus and the Tiber by Gabriele Valvassori. Near the orange plantation is the Fountain of the Lily. The lily and the dove are emblems of the Pamphili family; the Doria eagle appears on the Fountain of the Cupid and Angels.

Beneath the Fountain of the Lily begins a long canal cutting through the dense pine woods. Rusticated arches surmounted by statues and studded with busts frame a cascade over rugged rocks into the long canal. The cascade finishes in a small oval lake with an island, surrounded by the rolling meadows of the hunting preserve. Near this survive small structures for housing pheasants, red cows, a dairy, and an aviary, plus bird traps.

A small family residential villa with a loggia overlooking the road is tucked away in the northwest end of the garden by the walled orange grove. The towering rustic Fountain of the Dove faces the little villa. A private garden is just behind it.

Since 1963, Villa Doria Pamphili has been owned by the Comune di Roma, and its park is now open to the public.

Villa d'Este

Tivoli
Gardens open to the public
(closed Mondays)

Villa d'Este, engraving by G. B. Piranesi (18th century).

Cardinal Ippolito d'Este was a remarkable man of his era—a powerful prelate, a member of the ruling house of Ferrara and a patron of the arts. He was also skilled in diplomacy with strong ties to the French court, and possessed of unlimited ambition. Admired and feared in Rome, he was given the governorship of Tivoli and its territories as compensation for swinging his votes in the conclave that elected Julius III. Later, Paul IV temporarily deprived him of the post, under the accusation of simony. Although he had two villas in Rome and an establishment at Fontainebleau, he decided to transform the former Benedictine abbey at Tivoli into a grand residence. With interruptions, the work progressed from 1550 until his death in 1572. The garden was famed throughout Europe before its completion. One of the reasons he accepted the appointment at Tivoli was that it provided the opportunity to plunder Hadrian's villa nearby for his own collection of antiquities. He appointed the Neapolitan architect Pirro Ligorio as archaeologist in charge of the excavations and architect of Villa d'Este and its gardens. Ligorio called in other experts for the fountains and the rebuilding of the villa, but personally oversaw every detail. Certainly the general layout, completed in Ippolito's lifetime, is Ligorio's own project. The gardens were intended as a frame for the important sculpture, which was later dispersed by Este heirs.

The principal theme of the garden was the link between the mythical figure of Hercules and the Este family. (The idea of family glorification in a garden had its prototype at Castello.) The Este family traced their lineage back mythologically to Hercules and Hippolyte. They were particularly concerned with the concept of Herculean strength and power: Hercules clearing the Augean stables paralleled Ippolito's Herculean task of transforming the Valle Gaudente, site of the gardens, and bringing water by constructing aqueducts which were tunneled through the hill. Furthermore, at the cross-path by the huge statue of Hercules on the main garden axis there was the choice of turning either towards the Grotto of Diana and platonic, chaste love—and by extension the Amazon Hippolyte's purity—or towards the grotto of Venus and carnal love. The iconography was muddied by later owners, who substituted the big statue of Hercules for one of Jove, and placed reliefs of his exploits around the Dragon Fountain. The statue of Venus was removed and a Bacchus put in her place.

The construction of the villa and its gardens was extremely costly. Whole sections of Tivoli were expropriated for the garden, causing hard feelings among the townspeople. Cardinal Ippolito paid one-third of the cost for the Rivellese aqueduct, which brought drinking water to the town; its reservoirs lie beneath the villa's courtyard. However, the water was inadequate for the projected fountains, especially for the Fountain of the Organ. And so the cardinal diverted the river Aniene and brought water to the garden by a tunnel 3,200 feet long. It supplies over three hundred gallons per second, providing the force for over twenty-three major fountains, and hundreds of smaller jets, making this garden unique.

The garden was intended to be entered from the bottom, by a side road of the Via Tiburtina leading to Rome. The visitor looked across the flat portion of the garden, through the Rotonda, across the fishponds, and up

the steep hillside to the massive villa above. This is the view Piranesi drew. Today the myrtle hedges are much overgrown, and the effect is of a forested rather than manicured slope. The cardinal's state rooms lead out to a double loggia with sweeping views of the garden below, the town with the church of San Pietro and the countryside spreading in the distance. The lower loggia opens directly onto the broad terrace with its projecting belvedere over the hillside. The villa itself is set at a slight angle to the axis of the garden. Ligorio compensated for this by use of oblique intersecting cross-paths that bisect the major transversal paths of the One Hundred Fountains and the Cardinal's Walk. In this manner the steep hillside is crisscrossed in a grid pattern.

Today one enters the garden at the top, passing through the villa. On the upper terrace the belvedere overhangs the Fountain of Minerva. Its antique statues of Pandora and Minerva are now in the Museo Capitolino.

A left turn leads to the Grotto of Diana. The ceiling is ornamented with mosaic and stucco work. Delicate stucco reliefs depict scenes of Daphne, Perseus and Andromeda, and Diana with Callisto and Actaeon. Caryatids support baskets of the golden apples of Hesperides on their heads. Fetching the apples of Hesperides was one of Hercules's Twelve Labors. The reliefs all reflect the theme of chastity. The statues of Hippolyte, Lucretia, and Diana have also been removed to the Museo Capitolino.

Returning to the central axis, ramps descend to the Cardinal's Walk, a favorite place for strolling and discussions. Between the ramps is Bernini's Fountain of the Biccherone, or "Goblet," enclosed by a huge seashell. This was a later addition of 1660–61 under Cardinal Rinaldo I d'Este.

Continuing to the end of the path to the right, one comes to the former Grotto of Venus, tucked within the area of the Tivoli Fountain. This was ornamented with putti and an antique statue of Venus, which was later removed to the secret garden adjacent to the villa. Its courtyard had trick fountain jets.

Further down at the next level is the Path of One Hundred Fountains. This sheltered, murmuring walk is the romantic part of Villa d'Este. Three channels of water flow the length of its path, symbolizing the three rivers of the Tiburtine territories. The top canal is ornamented with alternating fleur-de-lis, miniature boats with a fanlike spray of water, and the Este eagles. Triple tiers of water jets sprinkle down the entire length. This fountain is the creation of Ligorio. At a later date, ninety-one terra-cotta bas-reliefs illustrating the tales of Ovid's *Metamorphoses* were attached to the fountain walls. These have almost totally deteriorated and are hidden by lush curtains of maiden-hair ferns. Light filters through the trees adding to the fairytale quality of this walk.

To the right is the magnificent Fountain of Tivoli, also called the Fountain of the Ovato. This is the largest fountain in the garden. It directly receives the water of the river Aniene, and is the distribution point for the rest of the garden. Ligorio designed a huge *nymphaeum* arcade, which the visitor can traverse, passing behind the crashing waterfall, which represents the falls of Tivoli. Niches are filled with nymphs from whose amphorae water pours into the large oval basin. Above an artificial rockery are statues of the Tiburtine Sibyl and the river gods of the Aniene and Ercolaneo. Crowning the mount is a statue of Pegasus, referring to the Spring of Hippocrene, created when the hoof of Pegasus struck Mount Parnassus.

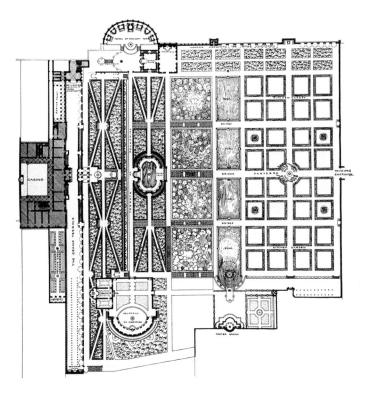

Allegorically, the "rivers" Aniene, Ercolaneo, and Albuneo flow through the Tivoli fountain, and along the channels of the One Hundred Fountains to empty into "the Tiber" of the Rometta at the opposite end of the path.

The Rometta is a semicircular stage on which is represented in miniature the city of Rome with its seven hills, dating from 1568 by Curzio Maccarone. Statues by de la Motte carved around 1607 depict a horse (Rome) struggling with a lion (Tivoli), and Romulus and Remus with the shewolf. The cascades of Tivoli are shown on the left, their waters flowing into a stream that runs along the base of the platform. In the stream is a boat carrying an obelisk, representing the Tiber with the ship of the Church. Much of the Rometta deteriorated and was pulled down in the nineteenth century. This area was used as a theater.

Near the Rometta is the Fountain of Persephone. In the deep niche seventeenth-century statues depicted the Rape of Persephone; she has vanished, but the figure of Pluto on his seahorse chariot remains. Twisted columns adorn the front of the grotto. In this century an ancient black and white mosaic floor has been installed before the fountain.

Originally there were statues of the four Roman emperors who built villas in the Tiburtine. The area facing the fountain was used for open-air dining.

Close by is the Fountain of the Owl. Enclosed is a courtyard topped with fleur-de-lis and owls; the lofty fountain is bordered by pilasters entwined with vines and golden apples. Elaborate stucco relief figures covered with mosaics have been restored. Putti support the Este coat-of-arms. The niche is now lacking its famed water-automated birds. Against a rocky

background, birds on bronze branches chirped until the sudden appearance of a hooting owl silenced their songs. Three statues of boys were seated upon an enormous vase, which poured water below. The surrounding niches contained fountain jets and figures of fauns and satyrs with amphorae.

Near the Fountain of the Owl is the Staircase of the Bollori (or "boiling" fountains). The balustrade ledge has forty-two low water jets.

Turning left one arrives at the centrally located Fountain of the Dragon, or Girandola Fountain. Twin curving staircases enclose a niche, which originally had the monumental figure of Hercules. The fountain has four spouting dragon heads, supposedly a compliment to the visiting pope Gregory XIII in 1573 whose family crest features dragons. The *girandola* or "chandelier-shaped" spray of the fountain produces a towering jet and was designed by the engineer Orazio Olivieri. This was the cross-roads to either Diana's Grotto of virtue, or Venus's Grotto of vice. Hercules was considered a victor over vice.

A staircase continues down the center of the garden axis to the third transversal path, the Hydrangeas, and down to the level portion of the garden. Here are three rectangular fishponds—four were originally intended. They face the dramatic Fountain and Cascade of the Organ. These fishponds once had crisscrossing jets of water, which created rainbows admired by Michel de Montaigne.

The elaborate Organ Fountain complex was not complete until the cascade was added below by Bernini in 1661. Gigantic herms guard the central travertine niche containing the Pavilion of the Organ. Flanking it are statues of Apollo and Orpheus. The Organ was built by Claude Venard in 1568, based on ancient descriptions by Vitruvius and Hero of Alexander of water-powered organs. It functions as water rushes into a cavity, forcing air out of the organ pipes. The keys are moved by another water driven device. First two trumpets blow, then harmonious sounds follow.

The fourth fishpond was never built below the organ. A Fountain of Neptune was to face the ponds but was only partially realized. By the end of the last century, only one jet functioned of the great cascade. In 1927 a new Fountain of Neptune was installed beneath the cascade. The roar of water is deafening here; the flat water of the fishponds lies in reposing contrast, reflecting the trees and tall jets.

On the main axis, at the farthest point from the villa, is the cypress-ringed Rotonda, which suggestively enframes the vista of the rising garden. Once there were flower-shaped fountains and antique statues of the muses in this spot. Originally this area was occupied by paths covered with *berceaux* and labyrinths.

To the left are the Metae Sudente—two fake rockeries that were intended to stand in the fishponds in imitation of ancient fountain goal posts found near the Coliseum.

Cardinal Ippolito collected talented men around him, notably the composer Giovanni Palestrina, the artists Benvenuto Cellini and Titian, and the poets Ludovico Ariosto, Torquato Tasso, and Marc-Antoine Muret. Muret's poems unlock the symbolism of the garden; he also wrote a number of theatrical productions which were performed here.

Cardinal Ippolito died in December 1572. The fountains were completed by his successors, who basically respected his original plans. The villa was willed to the cardinals of the Este family; failing a suitable heir it was to pass to the deacon of the College of Cardinals. Luigi d'Este inherited it. At this period the Este family removed all important statuary. When Luigi died in 1586 Villa d'Este passed to Alessandro Farnese who resumed work on the garden in 1605. Cardinal Alessandro managed to alter the will in favor of the Este family. Under Cardinal Rinaldo I d'Este (1633–73), Bernini and his pupil Mattia de'Rossi improved the water displays of the Organ and the Rometta.

The garden's decline began in the eighteenth century. Pope Pius IV at-

tempted to buy it, but calculated that it was prohibitively expensive to maintain. The last of the Estes was Beatrice, who married Archduke Ferdinand in 1787, thus bringing the property to the Hapsburgs. Under the Hapsburgs the villa was neglected. In the mid-nineteenth century Cardinal Hohenlohe rented it for a long period and attempted a partial restoration of the gardens. The composer Franz Liszt was his guest for several years.

Other prominent guests over the years included Jean-Baptiste Corot, Michel de Montaigne, Jean-Honoré Fragonard, and Robert Adam. Montaigne saw it in an unfinished state. He compared Pratolino to Villa d'Este, praising the beauty and ingenuity of Pratolino's grottoes, yet much admiring the site and the antique statuary of Villa d'Este. Only Charles de Brosses remained unimpressed by the fountains, preferring the sober, more finely finished creations of Versailles.

Villa d'Este introduced cascades to Italian garden design. The oval Fountain of Tivoli became the model for those at Villa Aldobrandini and Villa Lante. The concept of rectangular pools ending at a waterfall was echoed by Luigi Vanvitelli at Caserta.

Villa Aldobrandini

Frascati
Gardens open upon request:
Azienda di Soggiorno
e Turismo
1 Piazza Marconi
Frascati

Villa Aldobrandini was designed at the tail end of the seventeenth century with ideas borrowed from its predecessors. The garden is somewhat overdone: the sculpted detail tends to be coarse; the broken pediment on the roof line is exaggerated; the water theater looms up in uncomfortable proximity to the villa; the ascent of the hillside is abrupt, disturbing what could be a beautiful flowing entrance drive. Yet the use of a difficult site is brilliant, and the Baroque theatricality of the garden concept makes it memorable. In its original state it must have been an overwhelming sight.

The villa was begun in 1598 to designs of Giacomo della Porta and completed the year after his death in 1602 by Carlo Maderno and Giovanni (or Domenico?) Fontana. As with many Frascati villas, this is built against the hillside and is one story higher to the rear. The ground floor is visible only from the northwest front. From the rear, the rooftops of the ground-floor wings form a terrace level affording entry into the first floor, or piano nobile. The central block facing the water theater is composed of a series of loggias on an axis with the main garden features, beginning at the entrance avenue, which splices through the center of the terrace ramps. The axis continues through the house to the Atlas in the central niche of the theater, then up the cascade, via water channels to the rustic fountains and reservoir at the top of the hill.

The villa's entrance gate is located in the middle of the town of Frascati. The stone wall topped with vases is pierced with fanciful wrought-iron lilies—emblem of the Pamphili family, all designed by Cardinal Bizzaccheri around 1710. The long central avenue is flanked by two diagonal ones; each is bordered by trimmed laurels. Formerly this entrance approach was planted with parterres; now sheep pastures have taken their place. At the ends of the ramps are two large architectural fountains—tripartite structures with Aldobrandini stars set beneath projecting parterre gardens, which in turn have fountains with frolicking putti, and figures blowing water through conch shells on the balustrades. At the beginning of the ramps is a triumphal arch studded with fountain jets in the center and masks gushing water at the sides. The ramps surround an oval courtyard with a spacious triple-arcaded grotto. This area was undoubtedly the site of the lavish horse race of 1604 attended by Pope Clement VIII. From the grand terrace adjoining the house Franz Kaiserman painted a view of the town of Frascati and its surrounding hills. This little painting was commissioned by Goethe and remains at Weimar in his bedroom.

Behind the villa is the famed water theater with niches containing

over-size sculptures depicting Polyphemus with his reed pipes, a centaur, and Atlas (originally with Hercules assisting him—an allusion to Cardinal Aldobrandini aiding his uncle, Pope Clement VIII). Jumbled together are reliefs, Roman busts, and classical-style statues by Ippolito Buti set in two other niches. The central figure of Atlas, sculpted by Jacques Sarazin in 1620–21, holds up an enormous globe spurting water onto the moss-covered base. Flanking the theater are stairs to the balustraded terrace above, as well as various chambers including a chapel to San Sebastiano at the far left, and the Room of Parnassus to the far right. On either side of the theater are century-old plane trees planted in *quincunx* plan. More parterre gardens were beyond these; the one to the left is now destroyed. Charming boat-shaped fountains were also once found here. Stairways and ramps lead up the hillside to paths through the woods. In antiquity this wooded hillside was the sacred Grove of Diana. On this property was the site of the Villa of the Octavii.

The water for the Atlas has its source from Monte Algido. Fontana engineered the transport of water over a distance of eight miles to the reservoir at the top of the hill. The reservoir spills over the edge creating a waterfall between two huge statues of peasants set in niches. The flow of water continues down step-cascades to the crest of the hill behind the theater. Here stand two twisted Doric mosaic columns; water streams down the spiral grooves of the columns, and then joins the water rushing down the cascade to finally spray out of the globe supported by the Atlas.

Surely in its prime when the waterworks designed by Orazio Olivieri were all functioning, visitors took away indelible impressions of the

Cascade in the upper park of Villa Aldobrandini, from G. B. Falda, *Le Fontane di Roma* (1675–91).

thundering roar of the cascade, "Parnassus" or the Room of the Winds, and
the music-making statues.

A Latin inscription bands the top of the water theater; translated it
reads:

> After making Ferrara once again obedient to the Holy See and bringing fresh
> peace to the Christian Republic, Cardinal Aldobrandini, nephew of Clement
> VIII, erected this villa, arranging for water to flow here from Monte Algido, in
> order to withdraw to an appropriate retreat from his urban preoccupations.

The dukedom of Ferrara had been inherited by Cesare d'Este, illegitimate
son of Alfonso I. Refusing to recognize the succession, Pope Clement VIII
claimed Ferrara as a papal fief and sent Cardinal Aldobrandini there head-
ing an army to enforce his will. Cardinal Aldobrandini negotiated its takeover with Lucrezia d'Este, Cesare's cousin. She died shortly after her conferences with Pietro Aldobrandini; apparently charmed by him, she left
him her entire fortune enabling him to build the villa on the property giv-
en him in 1598 by his uncle Pope Clement VIII.

The Aldobrandini family was originally Florentine. Transferred to
Rome, the fortunes of the family soared with the ascendancy of Pope
Clement VIII in 1592. His nephew Pietro was created a cardinal the following year, and given the post of General Superintendent of Affairs of
State. In addition to the Ferrara takeover in 1601, he made peace between
Charles Emmanuel of Savoy and Henri IV of France. His tenure was short-
lived. His uncle died in 1605 and the new pope, Camillo Borghese, Paul V,
turned against him, revoking his position as vice-legate of Ferrara, and in
1610 put him under house arrest at the villa.

From old accounts, visitors to the villa were entertained richly and fre-
quently suffered indigestion. The architect Giacomo della Porta feasted
immoderately on ices and melons before departing for Rome. He never
reached his destination, dying en route. De Brosses and his friends, after
visiting the nearby Villa Mondragone where they got wet from the water
tricks, came to Villa Aldobrandini and, as recorded in his *L'Italie il y a*

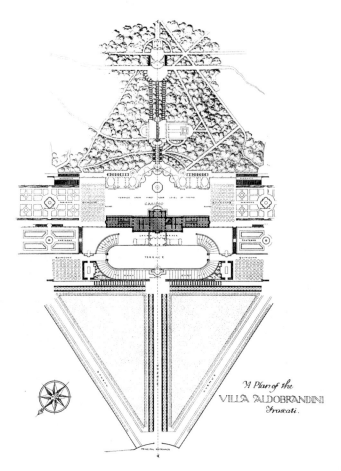

A Plan of the
VILLA ALDOBRANDINI
Frascati.

cent ans (1858), drenched themselves repeatedly with "one hundred little jets" in the theater, and on the stairways where the water sprayed the entire length from right to left. Legouz, a member of his party, ran to the top to turn on yet another valve, but was deceived, and soaked himself with a jet the thickness of an arm. "He fled with his breeches full of water running out into his shoes." Their supply of dry clothes exhausted, attired in their dressing gowns, they gorged themselves on several pounds of nougat and suffered severe nightmares.

After the death of Cardinal Aldobrandini in 1621, the villa passed to his sister Olympia, who married an Aldobrandini cousin. A trust established in 1611 protected the Aldobrandini name from extinction. The title of Prince Aldobrandini was assumed by Francesco Borghese early in the nineteenth century. The villa is currently owned by the Princess Aldobrandini. The villa was greatly damaged by bombing in 1943, but underwent major restorations between 1950 and 1960.

Villa Torlonia

Frascati
Gardens open to the public

Villa Torlonia was considered one of the three most beautiful properties of Frascati by the French magistrate Charles de Brosses in 1739. The garden, dating from 1623, is an early design of the great Roman Baroque architect Carlo Maderno. Its component parts have a potential grandiosity, but somehow seem strung together in an incoherent overall plan. The villa's location appears to be an afterthought, placed to the far right of the great staircase and off-center to the central axis leading to the cascade. The spectacular staircase is worthy of Versailles, but leads to a narrow terrace that extends the entire width of the garden, and is also out of line with the central allée.

The villa itself is unpretentious, its first story level with the terrace. This is not to deny the magnificent staircase. On either side of a cross-plan *rampe-douce* for carriages are two sets of double staircases, with low broad steps interrupted by paired landings. Elegant balustrades set with flower vases outline these flights. Pink roses grow in the intervening spaces.

The staircase terrace and the clearing above the cascade were designed as belvederes with sweeping views of the Roman *campagna*. Leading to the villa, a plane tree allée parallels the staircase. A thick wood of ilex looms up behind the staircase terrace. This is traversed by straight shady paths, once moss covered. Fountains play in rounded clearings within the woods. The central allée opens up into a large rectangular lawn facing a fountain-studded wall, which is divided into niches set off by pilasters with a large semicircular basin in the center. On a rocky mound a high fountain jet splashes into the basin, which also receives the roaring waters from the cascade above. Villa Torlonia's cascade has the loveliest proportions of those in Frascati gardens. It consists of three slightly graduated oval basins set against the hillside. Gently ascending steps are built against the contours of the basins on either side. These steps reach the summit of the hill where a round clearing is cut in the ilex. A balustraded platform extends over the cascade, and stone seats are placed around the edges of the clearing. In the center is a large quatrefoil reservoir with a central fountain jet. Its graceful undulating balustrade has masks facing inwards. There is a legend that the ghost of an evil monk appears here on moonlit nights, vanishing into the spray of the fountain and his watery grave.

The garden has links with antiquity, when Frascati was the city of Tusculum, rival to nearby Rome. Here Lucullus had his famed gardens and library. Afterward it passed to the Flavian dynasty and was restored and embellished by the emperor Domitian.

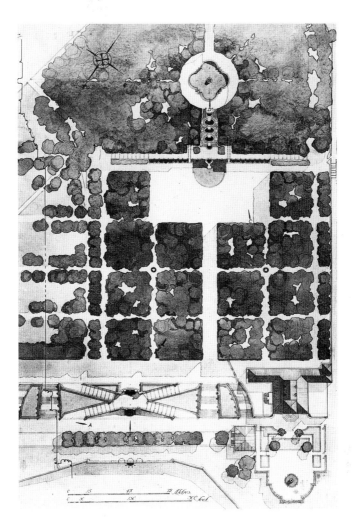

Villa Torlonia, watercolor by J. C. Shepherd (1925). British Architectural Library, R.I.B.A., London.

The property has passed through distinguished hands over the years. In 1607 the bishop of Tusculum, Cardinal Tolomeo de Come, sold the existing villa to Cardinal Scipione Borghese. It was later owned by the cardinals Altemps and Ludovisi. In 1632 the Conti family purchased the villa and created the present gardens. This family produced twenty-three popes and three antipopes, plus four saints and numerous other ecclesiastics and senators. The duke of Torlonia held the property until after World War II. The last of the Stuart kings, the self-proclaimed (1788) Henry IX, cardinal of York, lived here during part of his forty-two-year tenure as bishop of Frascati. Frascati was bombed by the allies in World War II because it served as German communications headquarters during the assault on nearby Anzio. Subsequently, "restorations" were done in dubious taste, installing jarring lampposts and lighting fixtures throughout the garden, replacing the mossy paths with gravel, and constructing a wide road for cars in the garden—all disrupting the beauty of the view and the serenity of the garden. It is now the property of the Comune of Frascati and open as a public park. The villa was transformed into a condominium.

Palazzo Reale

Caserta
Gardens open to the public
(closed Mondays)

Caserta, the swan song of the Italian Baroque, has a garden that was to have been patterned on Versailles, then turned full circle, reverting to the Italian gardens of Villa d'Este at Tivoli and Villa Lante at Bagnaia—a fitting reminder that the French classical garden had its roots in the Italian Renaissance garden.

Carlo III, ruler of Naples and Sicily, was first lured to Caserta by its rich hunting preserve, which he had confiscated from the duke of Caserta. In 1751 the king decided to transfer the entire capital to Caserta, twenty-one miles north of Naples, where it would be more protected from naval attacks and potential eruptions of Vesuvius. A plan was drawn up for a royal palace surrounded by an administrative city. In the mid-eighteenth century, Versailles was the favored model, to be surpassed in size and splendor if possible. The approach to the palace imitated Versaille's oval forecourt, as well as its three radiating access roads. In the gardens the concepts of a lengthy canal, formal lake, and an axial plan imposed on the entire park of 247 acres were all derived from Versailles. A discarded project by Luigi Vanvitelli dated 1756 which he published in his *Dichiarzione* featured large *broderie* parterres set out in colored pebbles or flowers, with a large central fountain, and an arrangement at the corners of this area cut into the boxwood hedges forming open-air theaters with diagonal paths. As at Versailles, "chambers" were designed within *bosquets* for taking refreshments.

Carlo III had visited Villa d'Este where undoubtedly he was impressed by the imaginative use of a great source of water flowing down a steep hillside. The straight channeled axis of descending water into a wider parterre area also has an ancestor at Villa Lante. A similar project is illustrated in Joseph Dezailler d'Argenville's *Disposition générale d'un magnifique jardin tout de niveau* published in 1709. The idea of descending channeled water set off from the palace by a terraced parterre was present at La Granja at San Idelfonso in Spain where Carlo III grew up, but here at Caserta the pleasing intimate proportions of La Granja, which gave it its charm, are distorted, elongated and overblown in an attempt at grandeur. On paper the design is undeniably spectacular; on foot, exhausting. The climax of the garden is lost in the haze of the distance. A horse-drawn carriage would be the proper mode of exploring the garden. The main parterre, planned to be adjacent to the north facade of the palace, was rejected in favor of a "river road." This is a continuation of the approach road to the palace, passing through a series of archways under the palace, and continu-

ing in a straight line to the beginning of the water stairway (or "river")
whereupon the sloping road branches and parallels the flowing water. High
cut hedges border the prospect and accentuate the length.

The massive palace is rigidly geometric, measuring 830 by 600 feet,
rectangular with four courtyards. George L. Hersey, in his *Architecture,
Poetry and Number in the Royal Palace at Caserta* (1983), sees the structure of the palace repeated in the forms of Vanvitelli's original design for
the garden: the garden paths, avenues, and "piazzas" akin to the corridors
and rooms of the palace; the interior ceiling designs reversed on the
ground in the garden rooms created by clipped hedges, decorated with
parterres, statuary, and fountain basins.

The king was a very active participant in the planning of Caserta.
Building continued for years, but he was destined never to sleep a night
under the roof of his palace. In 1759 he became king of Spain and left the
kingdom of the Two Sicilies, abdicating to his third son, Ferdinand IV,
who was then only a child of eight. Work on Caserta stagnated. Luigi Vanvitelli became disenchanted with Versailles and soaring expenses decreed a
paring down of flowerbeds; the great parterres flanking the pools and canals were eliminated. Numerous statues for the fountains were never finished. The triumphal arch was never built. The actual work on the garden
began in 1762. Vanvitelli continued to work on the project until his death
in 1773, whereupon his son Carlo kept up the construction from 1776 to
1779, during which the main fountains and the semicircular path on the
hillside were made.

Luigi Vanvitelli devoted much of his energy to an immense aqueduct,
the Ponte Maddaloni, which runs over twenty-five miles from Monte Ta-
burno, carrying an abundance of water to Caserta. The focus of the garden
became centered on this river of water, flowing through a tunnel to the

Briano hills, then continuing on a straight axis of almost three miles to the palace. Over the hillside it cascades fifty feet down to a waterfall, into the Fountains of Diana and Actaeon, underground to the Fountain of Venus, again underground to re-emerge at the Basin of Ceres, to triumphantly flow into the Pool of Aeolus, and hence to gush into the Fountain of the Dolphins. It was intended to continue to a Fountain of Neptune, and flow under the palace, proceeding by twin canals flanking the Via Appia to Naples.

Diana and Actaeon is a superb set piece in the style of François Girardon, consisting of a tableau of twenty freestanding statues flanking the waterfall at the foot of the cascade. These statues were carved by Paolo Persico, with Pietro Solari and Angelo Brunelli, between 1785 and 1789. The nearby Monte Tifata was sacred to Diana in ancient days. (Her temple was converted to the church of Sant'Angelo in Formis.) Diana, goddess of the hunt, was surprised by Actaeon while she was bathing with her water nymphs. To avenge this insult to her modesty, she flung drops of water on Actaeon, transforming him into a stag. Here is the moment of transformation: a stag's head surmounts the huntsman's body, and Actaeon's pack of fourteen dogs, no longer recognizing their master, attacks him. Legendary hunters are depicted in statues on the facing balustrades. Carlo III hunted daily as an antidote to his hereditary melancholy.

The following group is also a hunt theme. Venus takes passionate leave of Adonis, who is fated to die by the goring of a wild boar. Adonis refuses to remain behind despite the pleas of Venus. A platoon of putti enliven the group, clamoring over the rocks. When Venus discovered the corpse of Adonis, she sprinkled nectar on his blood, and in doing so the first anemone came forth—another example of the metamorphosis of a hunter evoked by a goddess, in this case creating a flower, a most appropriate theme for a garden. The group was created by Gaetano Salomone.

Water vanishes underground, to reappear in the Fountain of Ceres,

Palazzo Reale, from Triggs, *Art of Garden Design . . .* (1906).

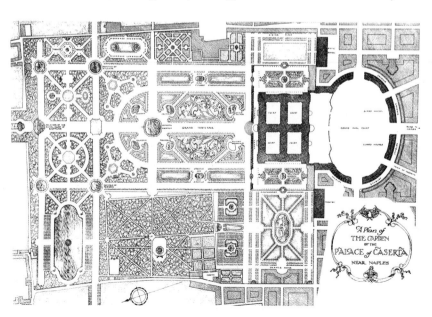

mother of Persephone, who was abducted under the earth in Sicily, to return annually for six months. Ceres is goddess of harvests and regeneration of crops. Her sheaf of wheat is missing now, but she still supports the large medallion representing the three-armed crest of Sicily. She is enthroned upon a sort of altar, flanked by nymphs and river gods, representing the Sebeto of Naples and the Vistula of Saxony, birthplace of the consort of Carlo III, Queen Marie-Amalia. (These rivers plus the Spanish royal rivers were originally to have been the centerpiece of the main parterre. Mythical rivers were to be represented in four other smaller fountains.) Tritons blowing jets of water from their conch shells are set in the basin below a low broad waterfall. This too is the work of Gaetano Salomone, dating from 1783.

The water flows underground again to emerge in a waterfall into a very wide basin. This was to have been the spectacular "Palace of the Winds," Fountain of Juno and Aeolus. The palace forms the background, consisting of an arched rusticated bridge, with a gallery within it. (A road crossing the garden passes over the bridge.) Figures of the winds tumble out of the "palace," spilling out onto the rocks. Planned, but unfortunately not executed, were large groups of Juno with her peacock chariot, and Aeneas with his ship, being blown to Italian shores despite Juno's imperious demands to Aeolus to carry him home to Carthage.

Following this is the Dolphin Cascade, consisting of a spurting sea monster flanked by two dolphins all spouting water—perhaps allusions to the creatures of the deep Aeneas would have faced. The intended finale was a statue of Hercules, the god who planted the Garden of the Hesperides in Campania—a fitting tribute to the gardens of Caserta and the ruling house of Spanish Bourbons.

More formal smaller elements survive in the "private" flower gardens on raised terraces at the east and west ends of the palace. The western garden is bordered by a vast orangery, the eastern garden is adjacent to a large riding area. Vegetables and apple orchards were formally planted with fitting statues of Pomona (goddess of tree fruits) and Vertumnus (god of changing seasons).

Deviating from the rigid plan imposed on Caserta, to the left of the garden's carriage drive is an irregular *bosco*, planted for a pre-existing seventeenth-century villa, its ancient trees untouched by Vanvitelli. Following a diagonal path, one comes to the Castelluccio, an informal retreat built for the young Ferdinando IV by Francesco Collicini, a follower of Vanvitelli. A moated octagonal tower must be traversed to reach its little garden, set off by a bridge and a spiraling ramp. This is a pretty parterred flower garden with three small pavilions: one for food preparation and another for its serving, the third for drinking coffee. The wrought-iron details have a Chinoiserie flavor. The moat was stocked for fishing.

The other "escape" is located to the right of the cascade of Diana and Actaeon. This is a charming English landscape garden planted in 1782 by an Englishman, Graefer, with a little pond and exotic plants, including magnificent magnolia trees. This was Queen Maria Carolina's equivalent to the Petit Trianon gardens of her sister, Marie Antoinette. Apart from these retreats, the garden was conceived as a vast majestic ceremonial backdrop for the court.

Caserta was taken by the Bonapartes, followed by the returning Bourbons, and then the House of Savoy, until it was turned over to the Italian State, which owns it today. The palace was selected to be general headquarters for the Allies in the Mediterranean during World War II. Here the Germans surrendered their army in Italy on 29 April 1945.

Glossary

Allée, Viale—a tree-lined avenue

Amphitheater—a semicircular wall embraced in the landscape, usually decorated with statues in niches and moldings; if it prominently features a cascade or fountain, it is called a *Water Theater*; if its architectural elements are in vegetation, it is called a *Green Theater*.

Aviary—a large cage or enclosure in which birds are kept

Balustrade—a wide rail along a balcony or terrace

Barco—a nature preserve for beasts and flowers

Belvedere—a building, or part of one, designed to overlook an attractive vista

Berceaux—a vaulted arbor or walk, either covered with trellis-work or by trees trained as an arbor

Bosco, Boschetto—a grove of trees, a small woods

Broderie—literally embroidery; the elaborate arrangement of flowers or box in a parterre

Columbaia—a dovecote; a building for sheltering domestic pigeons

Cordonnata—a flight of low steps

Espalier—a line of trees whose branches are trained to grow against a wall or trellis; also the trellis upon which the trees grow

Exedra—an open-air niche or apse

Giardino Segreto—a small, enclosed garden, often separated from the main garden for privacy

Giochi d'Acqua—water jets often designed to surprise the visitor; the jets also provide hydraulic power to move elements in garden display, such as mechanical figures

Hortus Conclusus—a Medieval, walled-in garden area planted with vegetables, fruits, and herbs

Limonaia—a green house for lemon trees

Mount—an artificially raised area at the end of a garden, often with views of the countryside

Nymphaeum—a grotto or structure with statues and fountains

Orangerie—a green house for orange trees

Orto—a kitchen garden

Parterre—a flower bed planted in an ornamental manner

Pergola—a colonnade of horizontal trellis-work supported on columns; an arbor

Quadrato—a garden area divided into four squares; derives from Genesis II: "and a river went out of Eden to water the garden; and from thence it was parted and became into four heads"

Quincunx—an illusionistic planting of trees in opposing blank rows

Ragnaia—thickets to net small birds

Spugne—artificial texturing of grotto walls, usually of pumice, stone, or cement, in imitation of stalactites

Stanzone—a shelter for wintering citrus plants

Topiary—plants trimmed or cut in unnatural forms

Treillage—trellis- or lattice-work

Vigna—an unpretentious villa with a rustic garden

Viridarium—an Imperial Roman garden, usually including a pool adjacent to the house

Bibliography

Brosses, Charles de. *L'Italie il y a cent ans ou lettres écrites d'Italie à quelques amis en 1739 et 1740.* Paris, 1858.

Burnet, Gilbert. *Some Letters containing an account of what seemed remarkable in Switzerland, Italy, in the years 1685 and 1686.* Rev. ed. New Hampshire, 1972.

Dami, Luigi. *Il giardino Italiano.* Milan, 1924.

Evelyn, John. *Diary of John Evelyn.* Ed. E. S. de Beer. London, 1959.

Latham, Charles. *The Gardens of Italy.* London, 1905.

Masson, Georgina. *Italian Gardens.* Woodbridge, Suffolk, 1987.

Montaigne, Michel de. *Montaigne's Journey into Italy.* Vol. 4. Trans. William Hazlitt. London, 1859.

Platt, Charles Adams. *Italian Gardens.* New York, 1894.

Shepherd, J. C., and G. A. Jellicoe. *Italian Gardens of the Renaissance.* New York, 1925.

Triggs, Harry Inigo. *Art of Garden Design in Italy.* London, 1906.

Vasari, Giorgio. *Lives of the Painters, Sculptors, and Architects.* Trans A. B. Hinds. London, 1963

Acknowledgments

Special thanks to my family and friends who encouraged and aided me in the researching of this book; to Sarah Burns at Rizzoli who carefully edited the manuscript, for her patience and enthusiasm. Thanks to the Kunsthistorisches Institut in Florence for their assistance; to Barbara Farnsworth and the Hotchkiss Library in Sharon, Connecticut for tracking down books for me; to garden owners Signore Arvedi, Marchesa Ginevra Chigi-Zondari Bonelli, Anna Mazzini, Notario Gianneschi, Marcello Marchi, Counts Roberto and Giovanni Giucciardini Corsi-Salviati, Count Giusti del Giardino, Marino Salom, Luigia Bellandi, and Renzo Perugini; to Ivan Grotto and Rocco Carlotta in Turin and Avvocato Berio in Genoa; to Ferdinando Chiostri for information about Castello, and the Florence Garden Club for advice and the use of their library.

Index